Fun with Poetry

KS2

written by Betsy and David Maytham

CONTENTS

Contents i
Contents by theme iii
Contents by poetic form iiv
Introduction vii

Year 3 poems 2
- Alone 3
- *Annotated version of Alone* 4
- Black History Month 5
- *Annotated version of Black History Month* 6
- The Earth 7
- *Annotated version of The Earth* 8
- William Caxton 9
- *Annotated version of William Caxton* 10
- The Fossil 11
- *Annotated version of The Fossil* 12
- Kings and Queens 13
- *Annotated version of Kings and Queens* 14
- Multiculturalism 15
- *Annotated version of Multiculturalism* 16
- Law 17
- *Annotated version of The Law* 18
- Reflections 19
- *Annotated version of Reflections* 20
- Romulus and Remus 21
- *Annotated version of Romulus and Remus* 22
- The Eagle, by Alfred, Lord Tennyson 25
- *Annotated version of The Eagle* 26
- (Unnamed Haiku), by Issa 27
- *Annotated version of (Unnamed Haiku), by Issa* 28
- A Farewell, by Charles Kingsley 29
- *Annotated version of A Farewell* 30
- Wynken, Blynken and Nod, by Eugene Field 31
- *Annotated version of Wynken, Blynken and Nod* 32

Year 4 poems 34
- Guy Fawkes 35
- *Annotated version of Guy Fawkes* 36
- Memories 37
- *Annotated version of Memories* 38
- Rosa Parks 39
- *Annotated version of Rosa Parks* 40
- Freedom of Speech 41
- *Annotated version of Freedom of Speech* 42
- Light and Dark 43
- *Annotated version of Light and Dark* 44
- The Romans 45
- *Annotated version of The Romans* 46
- Friendships 47
- *Annotated version of Friendships* 48
- Choices 49
- *Annotated version of Choices* 50
- The Volcano 51
- *Annotated version of The Volcano* 52
- The Ballad of Elizabeth Fry 53
- *Annotated version of The Ballad of Elizabeth Fry* 54
- Hope is the Thing with Feathers, by Emily Dickinson 57
- *Annotated version of Hope is the Thing with Feathers* 58
- A Riddle, by Christina Rossetti 59
- *Annotated version of A Riddle* 60
- Love's Philosophy, by Percy Bysshe Shelley 61
- *Annotated version of Love's Philosophy* 62
- He Wishes for The Cloths of Heaven, by W. B. Yeats 63
- *Annotated version of He Wishes for the Cloths of Heaven* 64

Year 5 poems **66**
- Florence Nightingale 67
- *Annotated version of Florence Nightingale* 68
- Elizabeth I 69
- *Annotated version of Elizabeth I* 70
- The Digestive System 71
- *Annotated version of The Digestive System* 72
- Tolerance 73
- *Annotated version of Tolerance* 74
- Light Lines 75
- *Annotated version of Light Lines* 76
- Mother Earth 77
- *Annotated version of Mother Earth* 78
- Holding Your Hand 79
- *Annotated version of Holding Your Hand* 80
- Stand Up For What You Know Is Right 81
- *Annotated version of Stand Up for What You Know Is Right* 82
- The Hawk 83
- *Annotated version of The Hawk* 84
- The Ballad of Philemon and Baucis 85
- *Annotated version of The Ballad of Philemon and Baucis* 86
- Miracles, by Walt Whitman 89
- *Annotated version of Miracles* 90
- Love and Friendship, by Emily Bronte 91
- *Annotated version of Love and Friendship* 92
- Storm in the Black Forest, by D. H. Lawrence 93
- *Annotated version of Storm in the Black Forest* 94
- Eldorado, by Edgar Allan Poe 95
- *Annotated version of Eldorado* 96
- The Best Thing in the World, by Elizabeth Barrett Browning 97
- *Annotated version of The Best Thing In The World* 98

Year 6 poems 100
- Alphabet England 101
- *Annotated version of Alphabet England* 102
- Happiness 103
- *Annotated version of Happiness* 104
- In the Blink of an Eye 105
- *Annotated version of In the Blink of an Eye* 106
- Learning 107
- *Annotated version of Learning* 108
- I Don't Want Heaven 109
- *Annotated version of I Don't Want Heaven* 110
- Galileo 111
- *Annotated version of Galileo* 112
- On the Bust of Shakespeare, Holy Trinity Church, Stratford 113
- *Annotated version of On the Bust of Shakespeare* 114
- The Ballad of Alexander Fleming 115
- *Annotated version of The Ballad of Alexander Fleming* 116
- UN Convention on the Rights of the Child 119
- *Annotated version of UN Convention on the Rights of the Child* 120
- The Man 123
- *Annotated version of The Man* 124
- A Book, by Emily Dickinson 125
- *Annotated version of A Book* 126
- (Unnamed Haiku), by Murakami Kijo 127
- *Annotated version of (Unnamed Haiku)* 128
- Invictus, by William Ernest Henley 129
- *Annotated version of Invictus* 130
- Jabberwocky, by Lewis Carroll 131
- *Annotated version of Jabberwocky* 132
- Sonnet 27, by William Shakespeare 133
- *Annotated version of Sonnet 27* 134
- The Tyger, by William Blake 135
- *Annotated version of The Tyger* 136

About TT Education 138

Contents by theme

British Values

- Year 3

Multiculturalism 15
Law 17
Kings and Queens (on the subject of the history of the British monarchy) 13

- Year 4

Freedom of Speech 41
Choices (on the subject of support services in society) 49

- Year 5

Tolerance 73
Stand Up For What You Know Is Right (on the subject of rights and responsibilities) 81

- Year 6

Alphabet England (on the subject of the history of British society) 101
UN Convention on the Rights of the Child 119

Famous people in history

- Year 3

William Caxton 9
Kings and Queens 13

- Year 4

Guy Fawkes 35
Rosa Parks 39
The Ballad of Elizabeth Fry 53

- Year 5

Florence Nightingale 67
Elizabeth I 69

- Year 6

Galileo 111
Shakespeare 113
Alexander Fleming 115

Geography/Ecology

- Year 3

The Earth 7

- Year 4

The Volcano 51

- Year 5

Mother Earth 77
Storm in the Black Forest 93

- Year 6

In the Blink of an Eye 113

Spiritual, Moral, Social and Cultural Development

- Year 3

Alone (on the subject of helping one another and options for seeking help in society) 3
Black History Month 5
Kings and Queens (on the subject of the history of the British monarchy) 13

- Year 4

Friendships 47
Choices 49
Hope is the Thing with Feathers 57

- Year 5

Light Lines (on the subject of family relationships) 75
Holding Your Hand (on the subject of family relationships) 79
Stand Up for What You Know is Right 81
Miracles 89
Love and Friendship 91

- Year 6

Happiness (on the subject of healthy and unhealthy relationships) 103
Learning (on the subject of education) 107
I Don't Want Heaven (on the subject of spirituality) 109
UN Convention on the Rights of the Child 119

Science

- Year 3

The Earth 7
The Fossil 11
Reflections 19

- Year 4

Light and Dark 43
The Volcano 51

- Year 5

Florence Nightingale 67
The Digestive System 71
The Hawk 83

- Year 6

Galileo 111
The Ballad of Alexander Fleming 115
The Man 123

History

- Year 3

Black History Month 5
William Caxton 9
The Fossil 11
Kings and Queens 13
The Ballad of Romulus and Remus 21

- Year 4

Guy Fawkes **35**
Rosa Parks 39
The Romans 45
The Ballad of Elizabeth Fry 53

- Year 5

Florence Nightingale 67

Elizabeth I 69
The Ballad of Philemon and Baucis 85
- Year 6
Alphabet England 101
Galileo 111
On the Bust of Shakespeare... 113
The Ballad of Alexander Fleming 115

Contents by poetic form

Ballad
Year 3: The Ballad of Romulus and Remus 21
Year 4: The Ballad of Elizabeth Fry 53
Year 5: The Ballad of Philemon and Baucis 85
Year 6: The Ballad of Alexander Fleming 115

Image
Year 3: Reflections 19
Year 4: The Volcano 51
Year 5: The Hawk 83
Year 6: The Man 123

List
Year 3: Kings and Queens 13
Year 4: Freedom of Speech 41
Year 5: The Digestive System 71
Year 5: The Hawk 83
Year 6: Learning 107

Simile/personification
Year 3: The Fossil 11
Year 3: Multiculturalism 15
Year 3: Reflections 20
Year 4: Light and Dark 43
Year 5: Mother Earth 77
Year 5: The Hawk 83
Year 5: Love and Friendship, by Emily Bronte 91
Year 6: On the Bust of Shakespeare, Holy Trinity Church, Stratford 113
Year 6: A Book, by Emily Dickinson 125

Free verse
Year 3: Alone 4
Year 3: William Caxton 9
Year 3: Kings and Queens 13
Year 4: Guy Fawkes 35
Year 5: The Hawk 83
Year 5: Miracles, by Walt Whitman 89
Year 5: Storm in the Black Forest, by D. H. Lawrence 93
Year 6: Alphabet England 101
Year 6: I Don't Want Heaven 109
Year 6: On the Bust of Shakespeare, Holy Trinity Church, Stratford 113
Year 6: The Man 123

Rhyming verse
Year 3: Reflections 20
Year 3: The Eagle, by Alfred, Lord Tennyson 25
Year 3: A Farewell, by Charles Kingsley 29
Year 4: Light and Dark 43
Year 4: The Romans 45
Year 4: Friendships 47
Year 4: Hope is the Thing with Feathers, by Emily Dickinson 57
Year 4: Love's Philosophy, by Percy Bysshe Shelley 61
Year 4: He Wishes for the Cloths of Heaven, by W. B. Yeats 63
Year 5: The Digestive System 71
Year 5: Light Lines 77
Year 5: Love and Friendship, by Emily Bronte 91
Year 5: Eldorado, by Edgar Allan Poe 95
Year 5: The Best Thing in the World 97
Year 6: Learning 107
Year 6: UN Convention on the Rights of the Child 119
Year 6: A Book, by Emily Dickinson 125
Year 6: Invictus, by William Ernest Henley 129
Year 6: Jabberwocky, by Lewis Carroll 131
Year 6: The Tyger, by William Blake 135

Metaphor
Year 3: William Caxton 9
Year 3: Law 17
Year 3: (Unnamed Haiku), by Issa 27
Year 3: Wynken, Blynken and Nod, by Eugene Field 31
Year 4: Friendships 47
Year 4: Light and Dark 43
Year 4: Hope is the Thing with Feathers, by Emily Dickinson 57
Year 4: Love's Philosophy, by Percy Bysshe Shelley 61
Year 4: He Wishes for the Cloths of Heaven 63
Year 5: The Digestive System 71
Year 5: Tolerance 73
Year 5: Love and Friendship, by Emily Bronte 91
Year 5: Storm in the Black Forest, by D. H. Lawrence 93
Year 5: Eldorado, by Edgar Allan Poe 95
Year 6: In the Blink of an Eye 105
Year 6: I Don't Want Heaven 109
Year 6: On the Bust of Shakespeare... 113
Year 6: The Man 123
Year 6: (Unnamed Haiku), by Murakami Kijo 127
Year 6: Invictus, by William Ernest Henley 129
Year 6: The Tyger, by William Blake 135

Haiku
Year 3: Black History Month 5
Year 3: (Unnamed Haiku), by Issa 27
Year 5: Elizabeth I 69
Year 6: (Unnamed Haiku), by Murakami Kijo 127

Sonnet
Year 5: Holding Your 79
Year 6: Happiness 103
Year 6: Sonnet 27, by William Shakespeare 133

Clerihew
Year 5: Florence Nightingale 67
Year 6: Galileo 111

Acrostic
Year 3: The Fossil 11
Year 4: Friendships 47

Kennings
Year 3: The Earth 7

Cinquain
Year 4: Choices 49

Villanelle
Year 5: Stand Up for What You Know is Right 81

Prose
Year 6: In the Blink of an Eye 105

Alphabet poem
Year 6: Alphabet England 101

Rap
Year 6: UN Convention on the Rights of the Child 119

Tetractys
Year 3: Law 17

Kyrielle
Year 4: Memories 37

Limerick
Year 4: Rosa Parks 39

SO HOW DOES FUN WITH POETRY WORK?

Fun with Poetry is part of our 'Fun with...' teacher resource series, aimed at supporting primary teachers. This book, underpinned by the 'Path to Success' and my 'Gamification for Learning' (see 'Introduction') provides teachers with a series of model poetry texts, across a range of poetry forms for every year group across the primary school range.

The poems have been written to specifically to fit in with topics that often are taught in primary schools. They are designed to provide teachers with a 'WAGOLL' (What A Good One Looks Like) to support the teaching of different text types. The poems are intended to spark discussions and creative thought. In my experience, teachers often struggle to find appropriate model poetry texts, pitched correctly. If teachers don't have an effective model to use throughout the teaching sequence, the outcome for the children is naturally going to be ineffective too.

With ever-increasing expectations of children's reading and writing development, the challenge for the twenty-first century teacher is to find a model text which not only engages the child, but also contains suitable language features, appropriate content and detail, and appropriately pitched vocabulary, grammar and punctuation.

Each poem has been expertly written and analyzed for you, to support you with identifying the key features underpinning particular poems. Each poem is extensively annotated for you, the teacher (not the child). These annotations are more detailed than would usually be necessary for the year group, so you can feel secure in your understanding of the poem and can teach it confidently. There are also some hints and ideas for discussions or activities you could carry out with your children within the annotations on each poem. (These are intended to be suggestions only and are by no means the only ways you can use the poems.)

Poetry analysis is necessarily subjective. We have given ideas and suggestions as to what the poems may mean. That doesn't mean that there aren't other interpretations of meanings or connotations that could be drawn out of the poem – you should feel confident to expand on what we have said and not feel constrained in any way.

In addition to the new poems, we have also included a number of classic poems. These have been put into sections based on our evaluation of their difficulty, in terms of vocabulary and theme. There are also annotated versions of each of these classic poems, with information about the poet, his or her life and works, and the specific poem in question, to support teachers in ensuring children recognize and appreciate our rich literary heritage.

All the poems in this book have been placed in year group sets. However, there is no need to keep them in these year groups. The analysis is appropriate to any year group and the topics may overlap year groups too. There may be certain trickier grammatical constructions in the poems chosen for the older year groups, but it is entirely up to you as the class teacher to decide what is appropriate for your class.

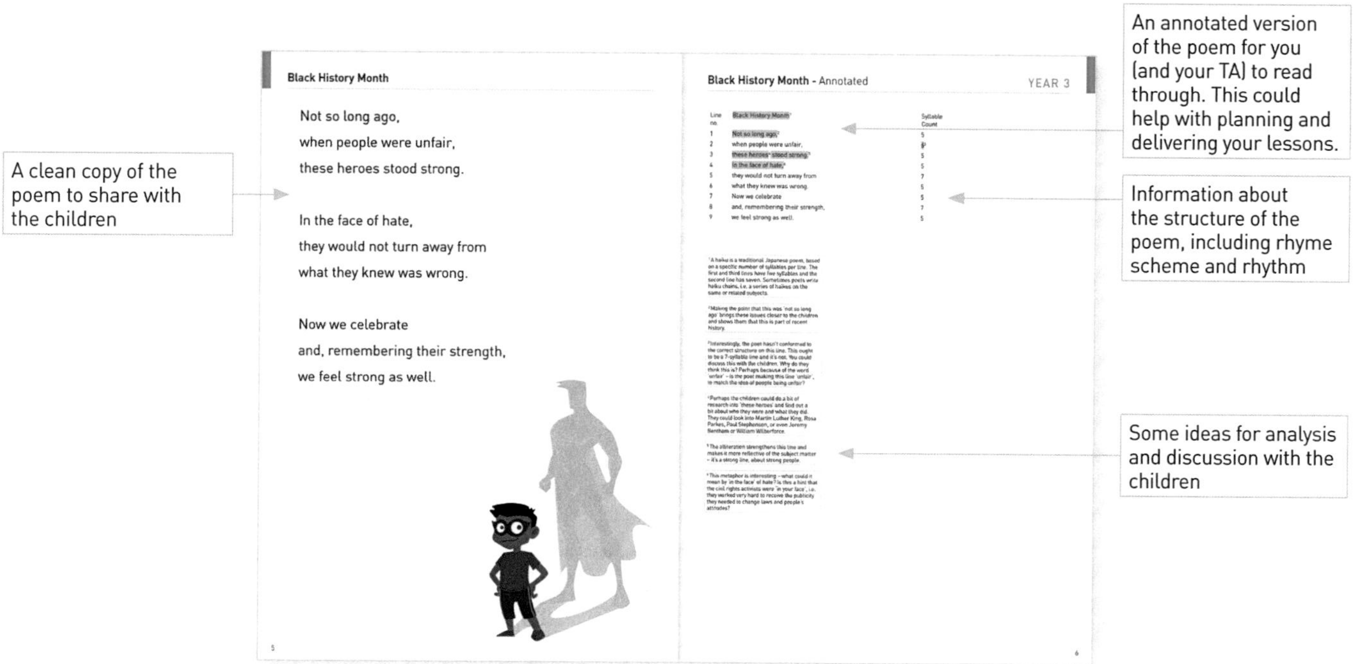

INTRODUCTION

Generating Ideas

A key principle of writing that I have always stood by is that you can't teach children to write until you first teach them to generate ideas. When you take some time to reflect on this, it makes a great deal of sense. I can still remember very clearly back to an incident that occurred in my early school years. I sat in the classroom, faced with the old style chalkboard and desks in rows. I was about six years old and my teacher asked me to write a story about a ship. I can still remember the wave of fear and panic that built up inside as I gazed at the blank sheet of paper in front of me: I just didn't know what to write or even where to start.

This experience is one that still rings true today. Although chalkboards are now mostly gone, having been replaced with Interactive Whiteboards and Smart TVs, I still watch lessons where children experience both this fear of starting to write (or 'Blank Page Syndrome', as the cool kids are calling it these days) and a lack of confidence in generating ideas for themselves.

Idea generation is a crucial and oft-forgotten part of the writing process. I would argue that a fantastic vehicle through which to teach children to generate ideas is poetry. Through poetry, we can experiment with language, play creative word games, test out vocabulary and explore language patterns in a fun, engaging and innovative way.

Unfortunately, in my experience, if there is any unit that often slides off the edge of the curriculum (because of the pressure of time or sometimes because of teacher subject knowledge), it's poetry. Yet this is one of the worst things we can do. I always encourage schools to design their curricula so that they start every new topic with at least a few days of poetry, and use the vocabulary and ideas they have generated and experienced to support both fiction and non-fiction writing.

The Benefits of Gamification in the Classroom

A key part of the path to success is gamification and active learning. The high quality teaching of poetry lends itself brilliantly to the gamification of learning in the 21st Century Primary classroom. Gamification is, I believe, a crucial part of of 21st century teaching and learning. It refers to the process of using the typical elements and components of games within what have traditionally been non-gaming situations, concepts or experiences.

- Games provide a **safe, unthreatening, familiar** environment for children to experiment and explore ideas and concepts.
- Games **promote repetition** – children will play games over and over again. It's through constant repetition that children will internalize the language patterns and structures necessary for them to become successful writers and learners.
- Through games you can provide **challenges** and an element of **competition**.
- Games can be designed to be both active and **engaging**. Time limits are important; they provide both a sense of urgency and competition.
- Games help foster **high quality dialogue** and discussion.
- Games encourage **collaboration** to achieve shared goals
- Games allow you to **simplify complexity** – often grammar that is difficult for children to understand can be simplified and easily understood through games.

In addition, using the language of the 'games' is as important as the games themselves. If you call something a game, children will begin believe it is a game and respond accordingly. A great example of this in action is playing word association games.

By providing children with 60-second idea generation games/challenges daily they will quickly improve their writing fluency, confidence and ability to generate ideas for themselves.

The starting point should be to give the children a word or high quality image linked to your topic and get them to write down as many ideas or words as they can in 60 seconds to do with that word. To start with, there is no need to target specific word classes.

The key is that you create a collaborative learning climate, where all children feel valued. Crucially, when playing the game, the teacher and, if possible, the TA should be positioned alongside the children as writers, so you go through the process with your children. When you first play this sort of game with your children, they may well only get a couple of words and they may have been borrowed these from you. However, if you play these games on a daily basis, they will very quickly move from borrowing ideas from you to generating ideas for themselves.

It is also vital that you model the process alongside the children. You provide time limits to engage and excite, and you promote collaboration and sharing to remove fear and set mini competitions such as 'can we beat the class record/the teacher?' and once they get the concept, you can then vary the games to focus on anything from figurative language to specific sentence types etc..

In schools I work with, who implement these sorts of games on a daily basis, it is not uncommon for the majority of year 2 children to generate around 20 words in a minute (from a single word stimulus), with the majority of year 5 children generating at least 30 words. The goal is to ensure that, no matter what task is now thrown at them, the children know how to generate those initial ideas for themselves.

The Path To Success in Poetry

The Path to Success is a forward-thinking, innovative approach to teaching and learning in the twenty-first century classroom, and can be applied across all subjects to support all primary schools in achieving outstanding results through engaged learning. The Path to Success is grounded in the latest educational research and first-hand experience of current teaching of real children in the primary classroom.

How is it different?

We are not advocating a scheme that primary schools, children and teachers have to follow in a particular order or predetermined way. In our experience, a predetermined scheme is unable to take account of all the various factors at play in any one classroom; including, but not limited to the skill set of the teacher and the ability range of the children.

The Path to Success is a circular methodology with talk, collaboration and active approaches at its heart. Its process can be applied across the curriculum, as the core techniques it embodies can be used to teach any skill or operation. Once teachers internalise this process, it has the potential to transform their practice and have a significant impact on standards.

What does it look like?

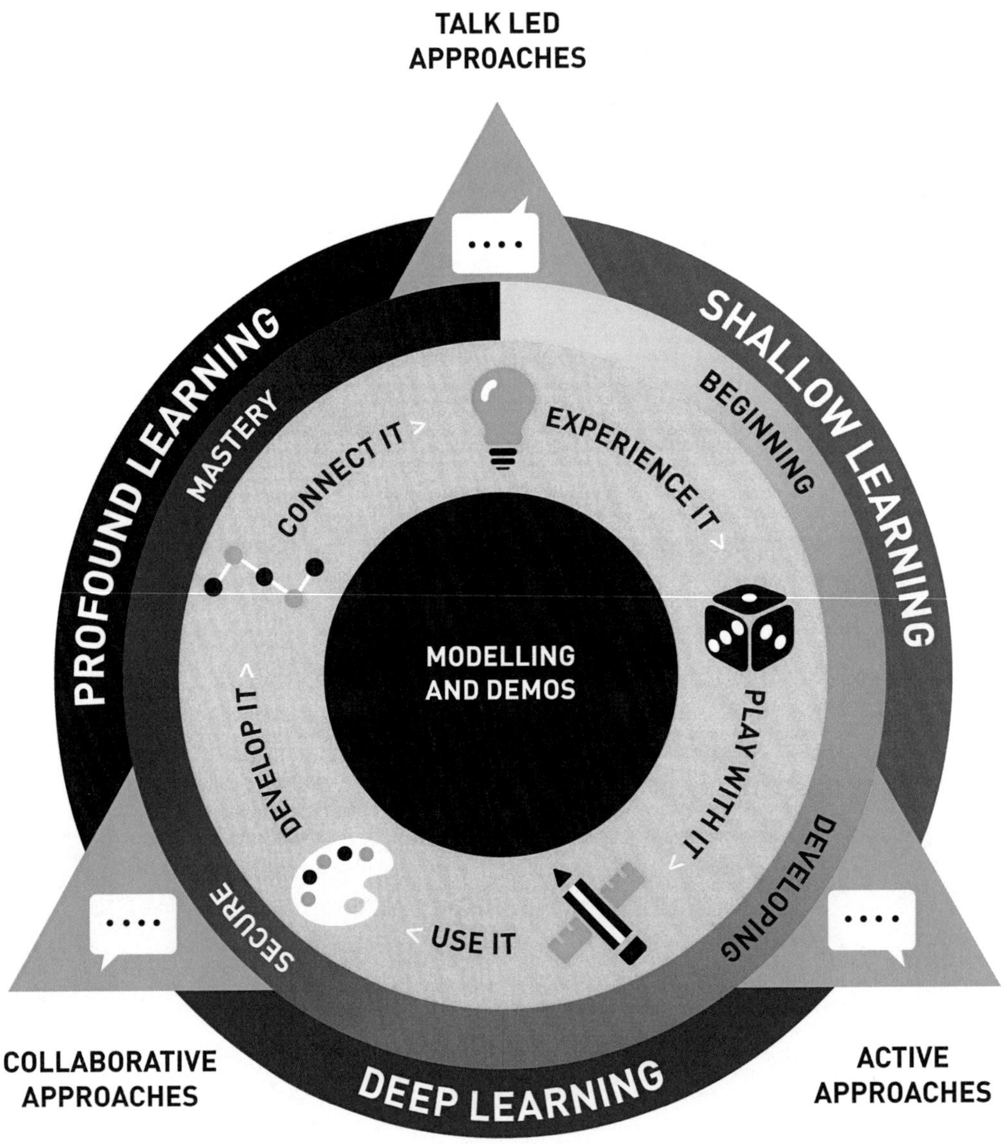

Teachers who use the Path to Success will develop and enrich children's ability to problem-solve, think creatively, improve their skills as learners and consequently make accelerated progress.

Stage 1: Experience it.

Children need rich experiences, which they can relate to, in order to support them in developing a particular skill set. For example, how can you expect a child to use personification in their writing if they haven't experienced it in any type of meaningful context? The challenge for us as teachers is to find a way to replicate this meaningful experience and practical application in the classroom. Personification is used in a range of poetry and narrative texts and is also commonly used in popular children's cartoons where objects are given human qualities. Providing children with a range of such examples and getting children to experience identifying and recognizing personification in context is a great starting point.

Stage 2: Play with it

This, in a sense, refers to the 'gamification' of learning. The power of playing short games to practice key skills on a daily basis should not be underestimated. Not only do they act as hooks to excite, engage and challenge the children but they also support children in developing fluency in a particular skill. By playing games with (to extend the previous example) personification (perhaps asking children to match objects found in the home with human verbs to create examples such as the pen danced, the cupboard opened its mouth) children are practicing their procedural efficiency with using personification in a fun, engaging, unthreatening way.

Stage 3: Use it

Once children have experienced a particular skill and had an opportunity to play with it in order to fully assimilate the technique, they then move on to using it in context. Practical application in context is fundamental to successful outcomes for children.

"Tell me and I'll forget; show me and I may remember; involve me and I'll understand."

- Chinese proverb

Perhaps children could now use personification in the context of writing a narrative poem.

Stage 4: Develop it

Children continue to develop the skill in context. It is absolutely crucial that all adults within the classroom, and within the school at large, position themselves alongside the children as learners, actively engaging in the learning process. High-quality modelling and demonstration should be underpinned by an active, talk-led, collaborative learning climate. It is in this sharing of the learning process that children find the inspiration to move from learners to teachers – if this move has been modelled by you, as the adult, they will follow your example! As practitioners, we should be aiming to move all our children into becoming teachers. If a child can confidently demonstrate the level of understanding necessary for them to be able to explain and teach a concept, idea or approach to another child, then in doing so they are demonstrating that their initial learning has been internalised and embedded. By this stage they are demonstrating a move from shallow surface-level learning to deeper learning and understanding.

Step 5: Connect It

This refers to children making connections across the curriculum. With a deeper understanding, children will begin to make links and connections in terms of how they could apply the skill or concept they have just learnt across the curriculum and in the wider world. Making these connections and exploring possible connections moves the child from deep learning into profound learning, which will stay with them forever. For example, children may begin to recognize how personification is used in narrative, or choose to use it themselves to convey a particular setting in story writing.

The beauty of the The Path to Success is that it can not only be used to teach a particular skills as outlined above using the example of personification, but can also be applied but can also be applied to the general teaching of a particular text type or type of poem. As an example, let's take list poems:

Experience it: Provide an example of a list poem, such as The Digestive System on page 71. Immerse the children in it. Perhaps compare it to other famous list poems such as Kit Wright's 'In my Magic Box' or Linda Knaus's 'Everything Pizza'.

Play with it: Gamify list poetry. You could play games or do activities such as generating list poems as groups, retelling them orally, performing sections linked to specific criteria, going on word treasure hunts or list poem bingo.

Use it: Ask the children to write a list poem linked to a particular theme or topic. They apply the skills they have used in the games.

Develop it: Children provide peer-to-peer support and feedback. They teach each other how to write a list poem and share ideas on future improvements.

Connect it: Children apply the grammatical structures, language, vocabulary and ideas across the curriculum. They use these structures in their writing for other subjects.

I would actively encourage you to follow the Path to Success and embed it within your schools teaching and learning policy. It is a proven model for good practice, which, if used correctly, will transform your teaching and your children's learning.

Below, you will find an example of a Poetry Learning Journey. This is one example of how you could potentially use the Path to Success to enable children to progress through the different stages of learning. This Poetry Learning Journey describes one week's worth of lessons.

STAGE			OUTCOME	EXPECTATION	EVIDENCE
Experience it	Day 1	**Hook** What is going to engage, excite and inspire the children to write? **Experience**	Children demonstrate what they know – they identify poetic techniques in model text. Identification of children's strengths and areas for development used to inform planning. Effective poetic techniques/ vocabulary/grammar identified.	Expectations for the week are written in children's books. Groups annotate large copies of the poem. Lots of talk and discussion of the meaning and the effectiveness of the language.	In books. Evident in planning as key teaching points and idea generation. Annotated copies of the poem up in classroom.
Play with it	Day 2	What experiences have the children already got? What experience has been provided during the hook? **Context**	Children are excited and enthusiastic about their writing topic. Children begin to use language in an interesting and engaging way – this informs their planning of their own writing. Teacher has provided a theme/context for the poem for the children to link their work to.	Lots of poetry games played. Attention paid to the analysis from yesterday – language created that fits in with the style and grammar of that poem. Children begin to idea generate for their own poem.	In books/writing journals. Photographs of children experiencing learning activities – stuck in books and an explanation written by the children. Daily hooks/games will be evident on learning walks, planning and in conversation with children. Evident in planning as key teaching points and idea generation.
Use it	Day 3	What is the background to the task? **Purpose** What is my ultimate purpose going to be? Display? Publish? Send to poetry magazine/ competition? Share with the rest of the school in assembly?	Children demonstrate awareness, and their prior knowledge and understanding, of poetic techniques. Using their experiences of the poem, games they have looked at previously and the context they have been given for writing their own poem, children write their own poems.	Language and ideas from previous lesson used. Children and teacher have a shared purpose for writing.	In books/writing journals. Visual prompts as supports for the children. Daily hooks/games will be evident on learning walks, planning and in conversation with children. Evident in planning as key teaching points and idea generation.
Develop it	Day 4		Children practice editing for effect and adjusting their language to fit the stated purpose. Peer and self-assessment of poetic language use.	Children and teacher have a shared awareness of the audience for their writing.	Evident in planning. Evident in the children's books.
Connect it	Day 5		Wider connections are made between the children's finished poems and the overall literature topic. Poems are shared and compared and discussed with peers and adults. Various activities could take place: group or individual mind-maps of topic; comparisons of the language in a paragraph from a novel/short story with the poetic language the children have used; transforming the text type into a non-fiction information/persuasive text.	Children's poems are finished – final drafts are now shared and discussed in light of the main literature topic. Language is used in a wider context.	Evident in children's books. Evident in planning. Evident in classroom displays (potentially).

You can see how the children's progression is clear, enjoyable and quantifiable. Using the Path to Success in this way ensures that children progress, while having an equal focus on promoting children's love of learning through gamification. The Path to Success, with its focus on gamification, should be used alongside the model texts in this book to enthuse, inspire and motivate your children, to support their development as poets and writers, and to ensure they have fun with poetry!

David Maytham

ABOUT THE AUTHORS

David Maytham

David is a former fast track teacher, education expert and school leader with a proven track record of supporting schools in delivering outstanding results. He was the Lead Writing Teacher at the first Writing Demonstration School in the country and has worked on research projects on behalf of the Department for Education. In 2012, David founded TT Education. He spends his time working with schools across the UK and internationally to raise standards. He runs training days, INSET days and national projects, as well as leading a highly creative team of teachers and other educational professionals to develop exciting and innovative educational resources for schools.

Betsy Maytham

Betsy trained as a secondary English teacher at the universities of Warwick and Reading and worked at schools in Berkshire and Essex before taking up her position at TT Education. She has worked for TT Education since its inception and has created course content and a variety of educational resources, as well as delivering training. Betsy specialises in developing creative and inspiring model texts and teacher support materials.

YEAR 3

Alone

When I don't know which way to go,
where do I turn?
Where do I turn?

When I don't know which choice will work,
what do I do?
What do I do?

When all the world is dark and I'm scared
and everything's cold
(everything's cold)

Who do I ask when I can't find my way?
Who will be there?
Who will be there?

I turn to you slowly, hesitating, anxious,
but you are so kind.
You are so kind.

I never thought I would be someone who needs you,
but I was wrong.
I was so wrong.

Alone - Annotated

A free verse poem is, in some ways, the easiest type of poetry to write. A free verse poem is a poem that does not have a regular rhyme scheme and does not have a regular rhythm.

Line no.	Alone[1]	Syllable Count
1	When[2] I[3] don't know which way to go,	8
2	where[2] do I[3] turn?	4
3	Where[2] do I[3] turn?[4]	4
4	When[2] I[3] don't know which choice will work,	8
5	what[2] do I[3] do?	4
6	[4] What[2] do I[3] do?	4
7	When[2] all the world is dark and I'm[3] scared	9
8	and everything's cold	5
9	[4](everything's cold)	4
10	who[2] do I[3] ask when I can't find my way?	10
11	Who[2] will be there?	4
12	[4]Who[2] will be there?	4
13	I[3] turn to you slowly, hesitating, anxious,[5]	12
14	but you are so kind.	5
15	[4]You are so kind.	4
16	I[3] never thought I would be someone who needs you,	12
17	but I[3] was wrong.	4
18	[4] I[3] was so wrong.	4

[1] Who is the poem written to? You could discuss this with the children. The point of this discussion is to highlight the fact that there are lots of people to turn to when you feel lost and alone. Why not ask the children to give some examples: Samaritans, Childline, school teacher/head/safeguarding officer, police, hospital etc.

[2] There are lots of question words in this poem: when, where, who, what. This sets the poem up straight away as one which asks the reader to consider lots of different issues. There is no detail given as to the issue that the speaker is facing – instead it seems more generic. This implies that the speaker is asking us, as the readers, to consider what sort of issues we might face and who/where we would go to find someone to help us decide what to do.

[3] The use of personal pronouns in this poem make it very individual, in comparison to the subject, which is very generic and lacks detail. Perhaps this is to create sympathy for the speaker – it's one individual speaking and worrying, so we feel sympathy and empathy – but to show that this could be any sort of situation.

[4] The repeated lines in this poem are quite interesting. Why is the second line of the stanza repeated throughout? You could discuss this with the children. Perhaps it's because the speaker feels stuck and can't work out how to move forward without help. Perhaps it's because the speaker is thinking the first two lines of each stanza and the third is what the speaker actually says to the person (s)he is addressing. Try reading only every third line of the poem. What effect is created?

[5] This pattern of three is significant because it's showing that it's not easy to ask for help – the speaker is acknowledging this. Why do the children think the speaker might not find it easy to ask for help?

Not so long ago,
when people were unfair,
these heroes stood strong.

In the face of hate,
they would not turn away from
what they knew was wrong.

Now we celebrate
and, remembering their strength,
we feel strong as well.

Line no.	Black History Month[1]	Syllable Count
1	Not so long ago,[2]	5
2	when people were unfair,	6[3]
3	these heroes[4] stood strong.[5]	5
4	In the face of hate,[6]	5
5	they would not turn away from	7
6	what they knew was wrong.	5
7	Now we celebrate	5
8	and, remembering their strength,	7
9	we feel strong as well.	5

[1] A haiku is a traditional Japanese poem, based on a specific number of syllables per line. The first and third lines have five syllables and the second line has seven. Sometimes poets write haiku chains, i.e. a series of haikus on the same or related subjects.

[2] Making the point that this was 'not so long ago' brings these issues closer to the children and shows them that this is part of recent history.

[3] Interestingly, the poet hasn't conformed to the correct structure on this line. This ought to be a 7-syllable line and it's not. You could discuss this with the children. Why do they think this is? Perhaps because of the word 'unfair' – is the poet making this line 'unfair', to match the idea of people being unfair?

[4] Perhaps the children could do a bit of research into 'these heroes' and find out a bit about who they were and what they did. They could look into Martin Luther King, Rosa Parkes, Paul Stephenson, or even Jeremy Bentham or William Wilberforce.

[5] The alliteration strengthens this line and makes it more reflective of the subject matter – it's a strong line, about strong people.

[6] This metaphor is interesting – what could it mean by 'in the face' of hate? Is this a hint that the civil rights activists were 'in your face', i.e. they worked very hard to receive the publicity they needed to change laws and people's attitudes?

1. Ocean settler
2. Mountain supporter
3. Desert smoother
4. Sky calmer
5. Breath giver
6. Space spinner
7. Joy bringer
8. Awe inspirer
9. Life creator
10. Miracle worker

The Earth[1]	Syllable Count
Ocean settler[2]	5
[2] Mountain supporter	5
[2] Desert smoother	4
[2] Sky calmer	3
Breath giver[3]	3
Space spinner	3
Joy bringer	3
Awe inspirer	4
Life creator	4
Miracle worker	5

[1] A kennings is a two-word phrase which describes an object or idea. It is essentially a very shortened form of metaphor, dating back to Anglo-Saxon and Norse poetry. A kennings poem is a poem made up of these two-word phrases, each used to describe the same thing. This builds up a detailed metaphorical picture of the object in question.

[2] The first four lines of this poem refer to specific aspects of the earth: features that can be found within the world, i.e. ocean, mountain, desert, sky. This grounds us (pardon the pun) in our subject – as readers, we begin to understand what the speaker is talking about, as this is essentially a basic description of the earth. You could ask the children to draw a picture based on one or all of these. Or perhaps they could see what other features of the earth they could come up with and how they would describe the earth using those features plus one other word.

[3] The final six lines of this poem refer to the more abstract features of the earth, moving from specific features to overall descriptions. Again, you could ask the children to come up with other abstract qualities of the earth or generic functions of the earth and then find a way to create a kennings from them. Or perhaps they could take one as a title for their own poem or story. You could ask the children which they like the best and ask them to discuss why and then write a letter to the poet explaining their reasons for choosing that description...or if they prefer their own ideas, they could write that in the letter too. You could send the letters to us at TT Education! We'd love to read them.

William Caxton

He unleashed a river upon England.
A broad, seeping, river,
which split off into streams and brooks,
leaking into people's heads
and watering their fertile minds.

With every sputter and grind
of his press,
it dripped knowledge,
information,
imagination,
into England.

No longer was this water source dried up,
guarded jealously by powerful men.
Now it gushed freely and joyfully
through narrow lanes
and crowded streets.

It's funny to report, but I hear that it's true
wherever the flowing water went,
it grew.

A metaphor poem uses an extended metaphor (which runs throughout the poem) or a series of metaphors, usually to describe one thing or explain one idea.

William Caxton[1]	Syllable Count[2]
He unleashed a river[3] upon England.	10
A broad, seeping, river[3],	6
which split off into streams and brooks[3],	8
leaking[3] into people's heads	7
and watering[3] their fertile minds.	8
With every sputter and grind	7
of his press,	3
it dripped[3] knowledge,[4]	4
information[4],	4
imagination[4],	5
into England.	4
No longer was this water source[3] dried up,	10
guarded jealously by powerful men.	10
Now it gushed[3] freely and joyfully[5]	9
through narrow lanes[6]	4
and crowded streets[6].	4
It's funny to report, but I hear that it's true:[7]	12
wherever the flowing water[3] went,	9
it grew.[7]	2

[1] William Caxton (c. 1422 - c. 1491) was an English printer. He introduced the printing press to England (in 1476), and was the first English printer, as well as the first to print a book in the English language. He made books suddenly available to a much wider selection of people (previously, they would have been reserved for only the very richest, as nobody else could afford the high costs of having them engraved). Not only did he print over 100 different books, but he also translated 26 of them himself. As the English language was still evolving in Caxton's day, Caxton was an important factor in standardising it – he would have been given books to print which were written in a variety of English dialects and he was the one who had to choose how to edit them into something which would be most universally popular. He popularised printed books, in his own words 'to the end that every man may have them at once'.

[2] You could argue that the irregular line lengths in this poem are representative of the flow of the 'water' it talks about. Sometimes the water gushes quickly, sometimes it slows and trickles.

[3] There is an extended metaphor of water as representative of books or knowledge running throughout this poem. The 'water' is portrayed as not only helpful, but welcome, exciting, joyful. This is a metaphor of something which starts at one small source, but increases, steadily and surely, until it gradually reaches everywhere – it is therefore really quite an appropriate metaphor.

[4] This pattern of three is powerful. Reaching across three lines like this makes each word stand out. Using the verb 'dripped' on line 8 to introduce the pattern of three, followed by the three words individually, broken up by line breaks and commas in this way, makes the words seem like drips, as if the poem is representing a dripping tap at this point.

[5] These adverbs are interesting. In what way could the children imagine the water to be 'joyful' and 'free'? Perhaps it's because people felt joyful when they had books to read. Perhaps it's because, although books were not free, suddenly they were more readily available. Perhaps it's because knowledge ought to be free, and that's what makes it joyful.

[6] Referencing both 'narrow lanes' and 'crowded streets' in this way implies that the books may have gone to both the city and the country. Narrow lanes are often found in the country, whereas streets in cities are usually crowded. Perhaps this could also mean that books started to become available to poorer people too, who might live in the narrow lanes, whereas richer people lived in bigger houses on crowded streets.

[7] The rhyme here, linking 'true' to 'grew' is quite interesting. It means that the poem ends on a rhyme – perhaps to indicate that Caxton's printing was a positive thing, as a rhyme is a pleasant thing; we automatically react positively to rhymes. It links the shortest line in the poem to the longest line. Perhaps this is to show that Caxton's books that he printed helped to link people together. Additionally, it's quite a sweet idea - that the water 'grew' as it travelled the country. What do the children think the speaker means by this? Could it be because the 'water' is representative not only of printed books, but also of knowledge, and the more knowledge people have, the more they can pass on to others and the more intelligent thoughts they can create.

The Fossil

Found in rocks and craggy cliffs,
Older than mountains and
Stranger than fiction,
Silently hiding for uncountable years,
I hold the secrets to
Life itself.

The Fossil - Annotated

Line no.	The Fossil (An acrostic)[1]	Syllable Count
1	Found in rocks and craggy cliffs[2]	7
2	Older than mountains[3] and	6
3	Stranger than fiction[4],	5
4	Silently hiding[5] for uncountable[6] years,	11
5	I[7] hold the secrets[8] to	6
6	Life itself.	3[9]

[1] An acrostic is a poem in which the first letter of every line spells a word or sentence. In this case: FOSSIL

[2] The alliteration here creates an aural image of the cliffs as sharp and pointy, with the repeated 'c' 'c' sound. There is also a 'c' sound in the middle of 'rocks', so you could argue that this is consonance (repetition of a consonant sound) as opposed to alliteration.

[3] Although this is literally true in some cases, you could argue that this is a metaphor.

[4] This is definitely a metaphor! And you could ask the children if they think it's true. What is strange about fossils? How do we feel about them? They could play a word association game or do a thought shower.

[5] What are the connotations of 'silent' and 'hiding' together? Do we feel as if the fossil is in some way afraid of the outside world? Or is it somehow threatening? The repetition of the 'i' sound links the two words together very closely.

[6] This adjective is an example of hyperbole (exaggeration for effect). What is the effect that it is creating? You could discuss this – how many years do the children think the fossil has been around? Can they do some research and find out how old the average fossil is? Perhaps they could write a report on their findings.

[7] This one, tiny personal pronoun makes this a personification poem. We suddenly realise that the speaker is the fossil itself.

[8] The personification and metaphor on this line are quite interesting – in what way does a fossil 'hold the secrets to life itself'? You could discuss that with the children – is it because a fossil is part of a scientific theory of evolution? Is it because it is ancient and has 'seen' a lot? It might be interesting to ask the children to write a story from the perspective of a fossil or from the perspective of the creature that created the fossil.

[9] This is a particularly short line. Is there a significance to this? Perhaps you could discuss this with the children. Having a very short line as the final line is interesting. Perhaps this is because it's such a large concept – there is a comparison between the length of the line and the content.

The English Kings and Queens

The list of English kings and queens
is the weirdest list I've ever seen!
Their names are strange – their lives bizarre –
it's hard to keep track of who they are.

Egbert, Aethelwulf and Aethelbald
were the first Saxon kings of the England of old.
And, though their names aren't often said,
next came Aethelbert and Aethelred.
The Aethels gave way then to Alfred the Great –
the burner of cakes – who now sat in state.
Edward the Elder, his son Athelstan,
then his other son Edmund became the front man.
Eadred and Eadwig and Edgar came after,
soon followed by twelve-year-old Edward the Martyr.
Poor Edward's stepmother was not a great fan,
so she soon got rid of the helpless young man.
Sadly, her son (who was just ten years old)
wasn't quite up to the job, so I'm told.
Aethelred the Unready – now that's a strange name! –
had quite an unsettled time during his reign!
When Aethelred's son died (which didn't take long)
Canute took the throne, and then Harold came along.
Harthacanute was the next and the last
of the Danish kings that we have had in the past.
Edward the Confessor took over from him
and he was the last of the Saxon kings.
From there it goes Norman, then Plantagenet,
Wales gets conquered and let's not forget
the kings of the houses of York and Lancaster
(they fought Wars of the Roses - what a disaster).
Next come the Tudors, the Stuarts and then
the country goes kingless, then kings up again.
In 1714 came the Hanovarians.
They spoke no English, were seen as barbarians.
But soon they adapted and won over hearts
with their great love of music and all of the arts.
In the twentieth century, they changed their name,
to make sure it's clear that they're English, the same
as their subjects, so now they're the Windsors and that means
that we've reached the end of our list of kings and queens.

Well, what a long history our royals can claim!
There are some strange stories and lots of strange names.
Which is your favourite? I like that one too!
Which of these names do you think might suit you?

The English Kings and Queens - Annotated

A list poem is exactly what it sounds like – a list. It can be a standard list of items, people or places. It can include lots of repetition or rhyme, but it doesn't have to. Usually a list poem will include some sort of comment on the list – its significance or what it means to the speaker – and might have a twist at the end.

Rhyme scheme	The English Kings and Queens	Syllable Count
A	The list[1] of English kings and queens	8
A	is the weirdest list[1] I've[2] ever seen!	9
B	Their names are strange – their lives bizarre –	8
B	it's hard to keep track of who they are.	9
C	Egbert, Aethelwulf and Aethelbald[3]	9
C	were the first Saxon kings of the England of old.	12
D	And, though their names aren't often said,	8
D	next came Aethelbert and Aethelred.	9
E	The Aethels gave way then to Alfred the Great[3] –	11
E	the burner of cakes[4] – who now sat in state.	10
F	Edward the Elder[3], his son Athelstan[3],	10
F	then his other son Edmund[3] became the front man.	12
G	Eadred[3] and Eadwig[3] and Edgar[3] came after,	11
G	soon followed by twelve-year-old Edward the Martyr[3].	12
H	Poor Edward's stepmother was not a great fan,	11
H	so she soon got rid of the helpless young man.	11
I	Sadly, her son (who was just ten years old)	10
I	wasn't quite up to the job, so I'm told.	10
J	Aethelred the Unready[5] – now that's a strange name! –	12
J	had quite an unsettled time during his reign!	11
K	When Aethelred's son died (which didn't take long)	11
K	Canute[6] took the throne, and then Harold[3] came along.	12
L	Harthacanute[3] was the next and the last	10
L	of the Danish kings that we have had in the past.	12
M	Edward the Confessor[3] took over from him	11
M	and Ed was the last of the Saxon kings.	10
N	From there it goes Norman, then Plantagenet,[7]	11
N	Wales gets conquered and let's not forget	10
O	the kings of the houses of York and Lancaster	12
O	(they fought Wars of the Roses - what a disaster).	12
P	Next come the Tudors, the Stuarts and then	10
P	the country goes kingless, then kings up again.	11
Q	In 1714 came the Hanovarians.	13
Q	They spoke no English, were seen as barbarians.	12
R	But soon they adapted and won over hearts	11
R	with their great love of music and all of the arts.	12
S	In the twentieth century, they changed their name,	12
S	to make sure it's clear that they're English, the same	11
T	as their subjects, so now they're the Windsors and that means	13
T	that we've reached the end of our list of kings and queens.	12
U	Well, what a long history our royals can claim!	11
U	There are some strange stories and lots of strange names.	11
V	Which is your favourite? I like that one too!	10
V	Which of these names do you think might suit you?	10

[1] The repeated word 'list' here is a reference to the type of poem. Potentially, you could also say that the repetition makes these initial lines 'list-like', in keeping with the type of poem and the noun itself.

[2] The personal pronoun used here immediately sets up a 'character' of the speaker. The speaker's personality comes through at various points in the poem, both with additional use of personal pronouns and with interjections in brackets or dashes.

[3] All the names in this poem are historical figures or families. You could ask the children to complete some research on these kings/families prior to reading the poem, in groups or individually. Or you could provide them with some information, again in groups or individually, which they could then teach to one another. Potentially, they could also do the research after reading the poem. They could also look into the history of their own names, or ask their parents why they were given the names they have. They could choose themselves new names – or even make some up! This could lead on to stories based on the history of their names or with characters with certain interesting names...or even poems about their names – perhaps acrostics.

[4] This story, of Alfred the Great who burnt the cakes, is one which it would be nice to make the children aware of. The story goes that King Alfred was on the run from the Vikings and took shelter in the house of a peasant woman. She allowed him in and asked him to watch her cakes (which in those days would have been more like bread rolls). He was preoccupied with thoughts of how to defeat the Vikings and allowed the cakes to burn. The peasant woman scolded her king furiously!

[5] In this context, 'unready' means badly prepared. The king got this nickname because he was disorganised.

[6] Another story of which it would be good to make the children aware is that of King Canute. People often talk about Canute as the king who tried to hold back the tide. In actual fact, this is a misrepresentation. What happened was that Canute was so popular and successful that his subjects began to say that he was not just ordained to be king by God, but that he was actually God. Canute was a deeply religious man and he wanted to disprove this theory. Therefore he ordered the tide to turn back, knowing full well that it wouldn't, in order to show the people that he was just a man. (This story is may not have been 100% true, but it's a widely-held belief.)

[7] From this point in the poem, the names of kings stop and the names of the royal families/houses begin.

Multiculturalism

As spicy as a curry,
as colourful as a rainbow,
as hard to pin down as a cloud.

As loud as a vuvuzela,
as entertaining as a party,
as chaotic as a stampeding herd.

As co-ordinated as a gymnast,
as strong as a mother,
as unpredictable as a storm.

As delicious as a fruit salad,
as useful as medicine,
as fragile as a snowdrop in spring.

As blended, universal and necessary as air.

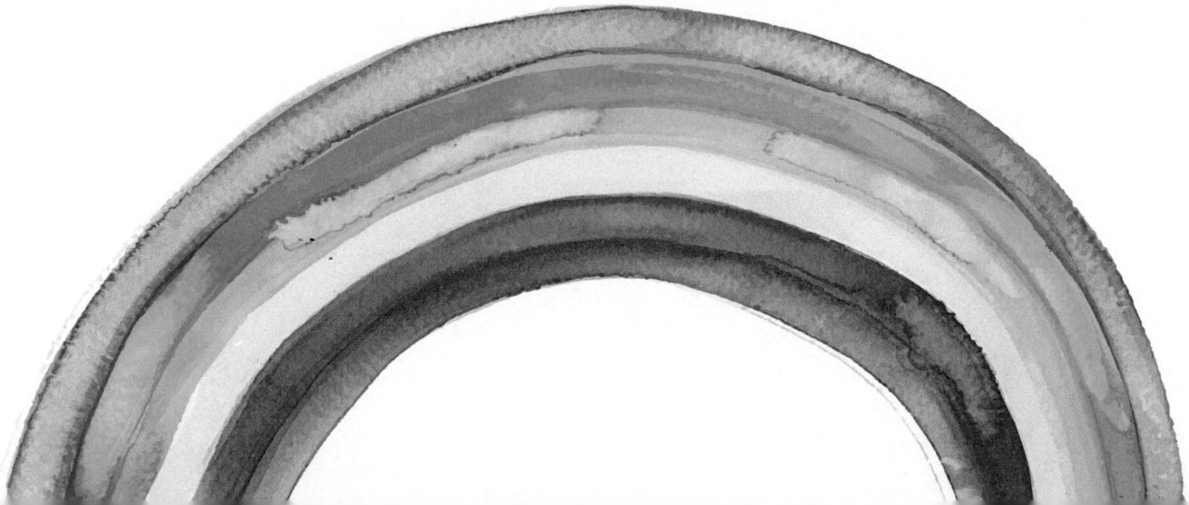

Multiculturalism - Annotated

Line no.	Multiculturalism	Syllable Count
1	As[1] spicy[2] as a curry,	7
2	as[1] colourful[2] as[1] a rainbow,	8
3	as[1] hard[2] to pin down as[1] a cloud.	8
4	As[1] loud[2] as[1] a vuvuzela,	8
5	as[1] entertaining[2] as[1] a party,	9
6	as[1] chaotic[2] as[1] a stampeding herd.	10
7	As[1] co-ordinated[2] as[1] a gymnast,	10
8	as[1] strong[2] as[1] a mother,	6
9	as[1] unpredictable[2] as[1] a storm.	9
10	As[1] delicious[2] as[1] a fruit salad,	9
11	as[1] useful[2] as[1] medicine,	7
12	as[1] fragile[2] as[1] a snowdrop in spring.	9
13	As[1] blended[2], universal[2] and necessary[2] as[1] air.	14

[1] A simile poem draws comparisons between the subject of the poem and a variety of different ideas, objects and/or places. This can work quite nicely if you ask the children to write a simile poem about themselves or about a friend or family member (as long as they're kind!) It promotes abstract thought and it's fun for them to guess who each poem is about (as long as they're kind!)

[2] Each adjective brings a new perspective to the idea of 'multiculturalism'. You could take them all out and give them to the children, either individually or in groups or as a class – perhaps you could ask them what they think the words describe (as a pre-reading activity) or to put them into groups, or to do an abstract drawing based on all or some of them. You could discuss the connotations – positive or negative? Are there any that stand out?

Law
is a
little word
that means a lot.
Our whole society, in three letters.

Law - Annotated

Line no.	The Law	Syllable Count[1]
1	Law[2]	1
2	is a	2
3	little word	3
4	that means a lot.	4
5	Our whole society, in three letters.[3]	10

[1] A tetractys is a five line poem which follows the syllabic structure you can see here: 1, 2, 3, 4, 10. A tetractys poem is based on the Greek tetractys, which is a triangular figure, consisting of ten points arranged in four rows: 1, 2, 3, and 4 points in each row (this is the geometrical representation of the fourth triangular number – a triangular number being one which counts the objects that can form an equilateral triangle). It was invented by the Greek mathematician, Pythagoras, and was very important to his followers, who saw it as a mystical symbol. It looks like this:

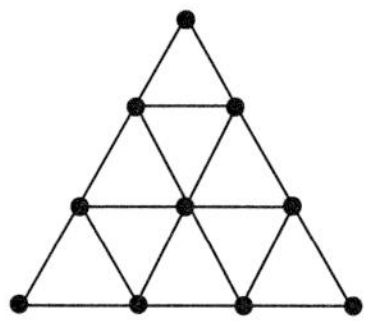

As you can see when you look at the poem, the layout of the lines looks like a triangle (not an equilateral one, but the number of syllables is a symbolic representation of the tetractys, because the first four lines – 1, 2, 3, 4 syllables – represent the four lines of the diagram and the final line has ten syllables to represent the total number of objects within the diagram altogether. We can reverse the number of syllables on each line (to make a reverse tetractys: 10, 4, 3, 2, 1) or make a double tetractys, in which you have a tetractys followed immediately by a second (often reversed, to create a diamond shape). There is no required rhyme scheme in a tetractys, but rhyme can make it quite an interesting form of poetry, if used effectively. The only requirement (and it's more of a strong suggestion than a requirement really) is that the first word (on the one-syllable line) should be a meaningful one, i.e. not 'the' or 'a' or something equally meaningless. You can see that this poem fulfills that criterion, as the word 'law' is the very crux of the poem

[2] Why not discuss this word with the children? What is the significance of this word? What does it mean to them? How do we decide laws? What is the difference between a law and a rule? Why do we have laws? What would happen in a world where there was no law?

[3] What does this line mean? You could link this back to your discussions of the first line. Is there anything else that makes up a society, other than law? Would the children disagree with this statement? The personal pronoun 'our' implies that the society the speaker is talking about is the one 'we', as readers, belong to. Is that British society? Global society? What does society mean? Also, can the children think of any other 'three letters' (or two or four letters!) that are this significant? You might consider things like: BA, jail, no, love, joy.

Reflections

The rippled river bounces the new morning light.
The clean leaves quiver in wonder at the sight.
The clear sky filters the sun to soft perfection
and all of it meets in a beautiful reflection.

Reflections - Annotated

This is an image poem. Image poems are really good ones to encourage the children to write, because you can be as supportive or as flexible as you feel the children need you to be and there is a simple start point for them to begin collating ideas. In brief, the children use a high quality image and write about it. However, they can use it in the sense of a very vague startpoint – 'tell me what this makes you think of' – or you can create a really specific set of criteria about the image – 'pick five features that you can see within the poem and use word association to come up with ten words which relate to each one...etc.' The poem can be super short or as long as the children (and/or you) want it to be. The idea of an image poem is to make children think really hard about their word choice. Does that adjective fully describe the real 'blueness' of the water? Does that verb fully portray the massive strength of the bird, if it should choose to move?

Line no.	Rhyme scheme[1]	Reflections	Syllable Count
1	A	The rippled river[2] bounces[3] the new morning light.	12
2	A	The clean leaves[4] quiver in wonder[5] at the sight.	11
3	B	The clear sky filters the sun to soft perfection[6]	12
4	B	and all of it meets[7] in a beautiful reflection.	13

[1] The rhyme scheme is very regular

[2] This alliteration creates an image of the river as restless and moving.

[3] The verb 'bounces' here links to the title of the poem – reflections. This could be an opportunity to discuss reflection with the children and how light 'bounces' off reflective surfaces. Can they think of any other reflective surfaces?

[4] The assonance (repetition of vowel sounds) here links the words 'clean' and 'leaves' together in a pleasing way – the sound of the poem is lyrical and gentle, just like the picture. You could ask the children why they think the leaves are clean. Is it because it's been raining and the leaves are washed by the rain? Is it because they're dipping in and out of the river? Is it because they're new and fresh?

[5] The phrase 'in wonder' emphasises the personification here, because you could argue that 'quiver' isn't really personification – it's used about inanimate objects often enough that it could be said not to count as personification any more. However, quivering in wonder is undoubtedly personification. The personification emphasises also how beautiful and wondrous the 'new morning light'/ reflection is.

[6] What does this phrase mean? You could discuss the meaning of 'filters' and 'perfection' with the children and decode the idea of the sunlight 'filtering' through the sky and shining softly on the trees/river.

[7] In literal terms, this is the case – everything in the poem 'meets' in the reflection, because the river is doing the reflecting, and the sky and the leaves and the sun are being reflected.

The Ballad of Romulus and Remus

Long ago, in Italy,
there lived a king and princess.
Their country was successful,
doing well at trade and business.

The king's brother was jealous.
A nasty little man,
he fought his older brother
so that he could steal the crown.

Her father gone, the poor princess
took flight and ran away.
She became a Vestal Virgin
to keep safe that very day.

The god of war (his name was Mars)
was watching all the time.
He felt sorry for the princess,
being locked up in her prime.

She was so strong and beautiful
that soon Mars fell in love.
He simply had to meet her,
so he came down from above.

Nine months after their meeting,
the princess gave birth to twins.
So Romulus and Remus's real
story now begins.

The new king felt quite terrified –
what if they took revenge?
He sent his servant out
to commit murder once again.

The servant felt so sorry
for the poor defenceless things,
he simply couldn't bring himself
to satisfy the king.

He put the tiny children in a
basket, safe and sound,
and pushed them down the river,
where they shortly ran aground.

A she-wolf found the babies
and she took them home with her.
She fed them, kept them safe
and kept them warm inside her fur.

Some time passed by and a shepherd
adopted both the boys.
They grew up poor but happy,
with dear love replacing toys.

As oft happens with children,
the boys turned into men
and soon they became leaders
of the shepherds in their glen.

Their band fell out with others
and a fight promptly took place.
Poor Remus was arrested
and the king looked on his face

and asked questions, till they realised
that they were relatives.
The king was scared but Remus knew
this wasn't negative.

Now Romulus came angrily
to save his captured brother.
Together, they removed the king
and rescued their poor mother.

The twins were each offered a crown,
but they politely said
that they'd prefer their own city
to rule over instead.

Their grandfather came back
to rule and he was very grateful.
The twins went off to found their city,
which turned out to be fateful,

for Romulus and Remus found
they just couldn't agree
about the new location
where their city ought to be.

They fought so long and bitterly
that things turned really violent
and in the end, poor Remus
lost and was forever silent.

So Rome was built, created by
poor Romulus alone.
Who mourned his brother sadly
as he piled stone on stone.

Here ends the tale of Romulus
and Remus, his twin brother.
Their legacy is Rome, the proud.
Their moral: love each other.

The Ballad of Romulus and Remus - Annotated

A ballad is a poem which tells a story. It is usually a love story, but not always. Ballads date back thousands of years and, in their earliest forms, were usually designed to be sung. For this reason, they have a fairly regular rhythm and a very regular rhyme scheme. The rhyme scheme is usually abXb, where X is a choice: it can rhyme with 'a' or it can not. Ballads are usually composed of four-line stanzas.

Due to the length of this poem, if you are reading it with Year 3, as suggested, it is probably sensible to focus more on generic points about the language and structure, rather than digging too deeply into individual aspects. If you choose to use this poem with an older class, you may want to analyse it more closely, but with lower KS2, the story is probably the most important aspect. Perhaps they could rewrite it into a prose story. Perhaps they could transform it into a newspaper artilce or an information text. They could draw out a timeline or focus on describing what they think the characters might be like (physically or in terms of personality...or both).

Line no.	Rhyme scheme	The Ballad of Romulus and Remus	Syllable Count[1]
1	A	Long ago, in Italy,	7
2	B	there lived a king and princess.	7
3	C	Their country was successful,	7
4	B	doing well at trade and business.	8
5	D	The king's brother was jealous.	7
6	E	A nasty little man,	6
7	F	he fought his older brother	7
8	E	so that he could steal the crown.	7
9	G	Her father gone, the poor princess	8
10	H	took flight and ran away.	6
11	I	She became a Vestal Virgin[2]	8
12	H	to keep safe that very day.	7
13	J	The god of war (his name was Mars)	8
14	K	was watching all the time.	6
15	L	He felt sorry for the princess,	8
16	K	being locked up in her prime.	7
17	M	She was so strong and beautiful	8
18	N	that soon Mars fell in love.	6
19	O	He simply had to meet her,	7
20	N	so he came down from above.	7
21	P	Nine months after their meeting,[3]	7
22	Q	[3] the princess gave birth to twins.	7
23	R	So Romulus and Remus's real	9
24	Q	story now begins.	5
25	S	The new king felt quite terrified –	8
26	T	what if they took revenge?	6
27	U	He sent his servant out	6
28	T	to commit murder once again.	8
29	V	The servant felt so sorry	7
30	W	for the poor defenceless things,	7
31	X	he simply couldn't bring himself	8
32	W	to satisfy the king.	6
33	Y	He put the tiny children in a	9
34	Z	basket, safe and sound,	5
35	AA	and pushed them down the river,	7
36	Z	where they shortly ran aground.	7
37	BB	A she-wolf found the babies	7
38	CC	and she took them home with her.	7
39	DD	She fed them, kept them safe	6
40	CC	and kept them warm inside her fur.	8

[1] The rhythm is fairly regular, to fit the song-like or chant-like ethos of the poem, so you can see that the number of syllables on each line are generally very similar. One thing you could do with the children is spot any particularly long or short lines and consider why they might be so short/long. Is there a particularly important message that needed to be given in that line?

[2] A Vestal Virgin was a bit like a nun – the princess has now become a priestess of the goddess Vesta. In many cases, the 'College of the Vestals' was a refuge for women in a similar position to the princess – it was a place of safety for unmarried women with no family.

[3] It may need to be specified to the children that this means that Mars was the father of the twins. Perhaps then move on to considering what this could mean. If they are the sons of the god of war, what will their personalities probably be like? You could consider other stories about people with gods in the family (as it were), e.g. Hercules.

The Ballad of Romulus and Remus - Annotated

Line no.	Rhyme scheme	The Ballad of Romulus and Remus	Syllable Count[1]
41	EE	Some time passed by and a shepherd	8
42	FF	adopted both the boys.	6
43	GG	They grew up poor but happy,	7
44	FF	with dear love replacing toys.	7
45	HH	As oft happens with children,	7
46	II	the boys turned into men	6
47	JJ	and soon they became leaders	7
48	II	of the shepherds in their glen.	7
49	KK	Their band fell out with others	7
50	LL	and a fight promptly took place.	7
51	MM	Poor Remus was arrested	7
52	LL	and the king looked on his face	7
53	NN	and asked questions, till they realised	8
54	OO	that they were relatives.	6
55	PP	The king was scared but Remus knew	8
56	OO	this wasn't negative.	6
57	QQ	Now Romulus came angrily	8
58	RR	to save his captured brother.	7
59	SS	Together, they removed the king	8
60	RR	and rescued their poor mother.	7
61	TT	The twins were each offered a crown,	8
62	UU	but they politely said	6
63	VV	that they'd prefer their own city	8
64	UU	to rule over instead.	6
65	WW	Their grandfather came back	6
66	XX	to rule and he was very grateful.	9
67	YY	The twins went off to found their city,	9
68	XX	which turned out to be fateful,	7
69	ZZ	for Romulus and Remus found	8
70	AAA	they just couldn't agree	6
71	BBB	about the new location	7
72	AAA	where their city ought to be.	7
73	CCC	They fought so long and bitterly	8
74	DDD	that things turned really violent	7
75	EEE	and in the end, poor Remus	7
76	DDD	lost and was forever silent.	8
77	FFF	So Rome was built, created by	8
78	GGG	poor Romulus alone.	6
79	HHH	Who mourned his brother sadly	7
80	GGG	as he piled stone on stone.	7
81	III	Here ends the tale of Romulus	8
82	JJJ	and Remus, his twin brother.	7
83	KKK	Their legacy is Rome, the proud.	8
84	JJJ	Their moral: love each other.	7

He clasps the crag with crooked hands;
Close to the sun in lonely lands,
Ring'd with the azure world, he stands.
The wrinkled sea beneath him crawls;
He watches from his mountain walls,
And like a thunderbolt he falls.

The Eagle, by Alfred, Lord Tennyson - Annotated

Line no.	Rhyme scheme	The Eagle, by Alfred, Lord Tennyson[1]	Syllable Count[2]
1	A	He clasps[3,4] the crag[4] with crooked[4] hands;	8
2	A	Close[4] to the sun[5] in lonely lands,	8
3	A	Ring'd with the azure world[6] he stands[3].	8
4	B	The wrinkled sea[7] beneath him crawls;	8
5	B	He watches[3] from his mountain walls,	8
6	B	And like a thunderbolt[8] he falls[3].	8

[1] Alfred, Lord Tennyson (1809-1892) was Poet Laureate of Great Britain and Ireland for several years in the eighteenth century. In fact, he held the position for the longest time of any Poet Laureate before or since (42 years). Born to a middle-class family, it was his poetry that gave him his baronetcy and entitled him to be 'Lord' Tennyson. Tennyson's output was so prolific and wide-ranging that it is difficult to limit it to a set of 'themes' with which he was concerned. However, he did write several poems to do with observations of the natural world. Additionally, he was very interested in poetic metre.

[2] This poem is written in iambic tetrameter. This means that every line has eight syllables, broken down into four metrical feet consisting of two syllables each. A metrical foot in poetry is like a bar in music – it is how we separate rhythmic phrases of the same length. There are four metrical feet, called iambs, in each line of iambic tetrameter. Each iamb is a unit of rhythm which goes 'da-DUM'. Thus, a line of iambic pentameter goes 'da-DUM da-DUM da-DUM da-DUM', where each 'da' and 'DUM' is one syllable. A word such as 'away' has a natural iambic rhythm, because we put the emphasis on the 'way' when we pronounce it, we wouldn't say 'A-way', we would say 'a-WAY'. If you emphasise the natural rhythm of speech when you read this poem, you will notice the iambic rhythm immediately.

There are two instances where the poem breaks this iambic rhythm. At the beginning of lines two and three, the rhythm starts with one trochee, which is then followed by three iambs. A trochee is the opposite to an iamb: it is one stressed syllable followed by one unstressed syllable (DUM-da). However, aside from these two breaks, the poem sticks to iambic meter.

[3] The eagle is only given four actions in this poem and all of them are passive. The speaker personifies the bird, with the personal pronouns 'he', 'him' and 'his'. However, the eagle is not named within the poem – only in the title. Thus we have an unnamed entity ('he') being passive. He just stands and watches, until he's ready, but even then, he doesn't 'swoop' in or 'dive', he just 'falls'. Could this be Tennyson talking about God? Tennyson did not have a strong Christian faith. In fact, he described himself as tending towards 'pantheism' (the idea that God is in everything in the universe) and 'agnosticism' (the belief that we cannot know anything about God). Thus, could this be Tennyson talking about a passive, watchful God, that is nonetheless within everything and seeing everything? This would make it interesting that at the end he 'falls' - the eagle isn't actually falling, he's not dying or anything - perhaps this represents God's retribution on sinners? Or perhaps it's a person's soul that is being discussed here; falling into death. But the fall of the eagle isn't sad - it's glorious and freeing.

[4] The alliteration here creates a very strong sense of the rhythm Tennyson is going for. Each 'c' word (even the 'close' – see comment regarding meter) is a stressed syllable. Using this alliteration in this way supports the rhythm and emphasises the words Tennyson wants us to focus on. Why would he want us to focus on these words? You could discuss that with the children.

[5] Literally, the eagle is 'close to the sun' because he is high up – on the 'mountain' that is introduced on line 5. Metaphorically, perhaps the eagle is close to the sun because it represents either a soul or God (as in the previous comment regarding the eagle's actions).

[6] In what way is the eagle 'ring'd with the azure world'? Is this a hint that the 'mountain walls' are on a small island and the eagle is ringed with water? Or is it talking about the sky? Either way, the adjective 'azure' implies purity, clarity and beauty and the verb 'ring'd' implies that the eagle is somehow at the centre of the world.

[7] This is an interesting metaphor. Why is the sea 'wrinkled'? Is this implying that the eagle is so high up that the sea looks like a piece of wrinkled blue cloth? Is this implying that the sea is old – or maybe even that the eagle is old? Perhaps all these meanings at once are what the speaker was going for.

[8] This simile contrasts to the passive verb at the end 'falls'. How can the eagle be like a thunderbolt, which is powerful and dangerous, when he is only 'falling'? Perhaps this juxtaposition is implying that although the eagle may look like he's just falling, in fact he contains power and energy which could be dangerous if we underestimate him.

A giant firefly:
that way, this way, that way, this -
and it passes by.

(Unnamed Haiku) by Issa - Annotated

Line no.	Rhyme scheme	(Unnamed Haiku)[1] by Issa[2]	Syllable Count
1	A	A giant firefly:[3]	5
2	B	that way, this way, that way, this[4]-	7
3	A	and it passes by.[5]	5

[1] A haiku is a traditional Japanese poem, based on a specific number of syllables per line. The first and third lines have five syllables and the second line has seven. Sometimes poets write haiku chains, i.e. a series of haikus on the same or related subjects.

[2] Kobayashi Issa (1763-1828) was a Japanese poet and Buddhist priest. He had an extremely hard life, losing first his mother, beloved grandmother, father, three children and his wife, followed by his house burning down. He is considered to be one of the four haiku masters in Japan and his often melancholy poems are extremely popular.

[3] What does the 'giant firefly' represent? Is it simply a big insect? Could it be a metaphor for the sun or the moon? Or perhaps a star – or a shooting star? You could discuss this with the children.

[4] The repetition on this line could represent the movement of the firefly – its erratic movements back and forth are represented in the repetition of the language used to describe its movements!

[5] This is quite an interesting phrase. The firefly (or the sun, moon or star) 'passes by' but what else could have passed by? Perhaps this is a metaphor for our progress through the world – it can seem erratic and stressful and difficult, but we get there in the end.

A Farewell, by Charles Kingsley

I

My fairest child, I have no song to give you;
No lark could pipe to skies so dull and grey:
Yet, ere we part, one lesson I can leave you
For every day.

II

Be good, sweet maid, and let who will be clever;
Do noble things, not dream them, all day long:
And so make life, death, and that vast for-ever
One grand, sweet song.

A Farewell, by Charles Kingsley - Annotated

Line no.	Rhyme scheme[2]	A Farewell, by Charles Kingsley[1]	Syllable Count[2]
1	A	My fairest child,[3] I have no song to give you;	11
2	B	No lark could pipe to skies so dull and grey:[4]	10
3	A	Yet, ere [5] we part, one lesson I can leave you [6]	11
4	B	For every day.[7]	4
5	C	Be good, sweet maid, and let who will be clever;[8]	11
6	D	Do noble things, not dream them, all day long:	10
7	C	And so make life, death, and that vast for-ever[9]	11
8	D	One grand, sweet song[10]	4

[1] Charles Kingsley (1819-1875) was a Church of England vicar, a university professor, historian, novelist and poet. He is best known now for his novels "The Water-Babies" and "Westward Ho!"

[2] The structure of this poem is very regular, as is the rhyme scheme. It could be argued that this is because the speaker is addressing a child – the sing-song nature of the poem is like a nursery rhyme, despite the serious message of the poem.

[3] The possessive pronoun 'my' implies that the person bidding farewell to the child is the child's parent. (S)he obviously cares a great deal for the child, as (s)he has used the superlative adjective 'fairest' to describe the child.

[4] Why are the skies so 'dull and grey'? Is this a metaphor – the sky is grey to reflect the emotions, because the parent has to leave the child?

[5] 'ere' = 'before' or 'as'

[6] The alliteration on 'lesson' and 'leave' highlights these two words – perhaps to make it clear that this is a valuable thing that the parent is leaving with the child in order to make the parting easier.

[7] You could discuss with the children as to why they think that this line is so short. Is it because the speaker-parent is becoming emotional and having to trail off? Perhaps it's because these are important words, which the parent wants to emphasise to the child.

[8] This line is rather controversial. It seems as if the parent is telling the little girl to be good, not clever. Is this an implication that girls oughtn't to be clever? This would be a very Victorian way of looking at it. However, juxtaposed with the following line, in which the parent encourages the child to 'do noble things, not dream them', perhaps this is an encouragement to DO something, rather than sitting around thinking about things. The parent could be implying that actions are more powerful than words and it's better to be a good, active person that a smart aleck.

[9] This phrase seems to be referring to heaven: the infinite 'for-ever' that Kingsley, as a vicar, would have probably believed was waiting for him after death.

[10] This is an interesting metaphor. How can life be a song? You could discuss this with the children. Perhaps it's because it's beautiful, perhaps it's because a good, hardworking life brings harmony to the person living it. Perhaps it's a reference to hymns and the parent is saying that a hymn is a song of praise to God, so a life well-lived is a song of praise to God.

Wynken, Blynken, and Nod, by Eugene Field

Wynken, Blynken, and Nod one night
  Sailed off in a wooden shoe,—
Sailed on a river of crystal light
  Into a sea of dew.
"Where are you going, and what do you wish?"
  The old moon asked the three.
"We have come to fish for the herring-fish
  That live in this beautiful sea;
  Nets of silver and gold have we,"
      Said Wynken,
      Blynken,
      And Nod.

The old moon laughed and sang a song,
  As they rocked in the wooden shoe;
And the wind that sped them all night long
  Ruffled the waves of dew;
The little stars were the herring-fish
  That lived in the beautiful sea.
"Now cast your nets wherever you wish,—
  Never afraid are we!"
  So cried the stars to the fishermen three,
      Wynken,
      Blynken,
      And Nod.

All night long their nets they threw
  To the stars in the twinkling foam,—
Then down from the skies came the wooden shoe,
  Bringing the fishermen home:
'Twas all so pretty a sail, it seemed
  As if it could not be;
And some folk thought 'twas a dream they'd dreamed
  Of sailing that beautiful sea;
  But I shall name you the fishermen three:
      Wynken,
      Blynken,
      And Nod.

Wynken and Blynken are two little eyes,
  And Nod is a little head,
And the wooden shoe that sailed the skies
  Is a wee one's trundle-bed;
So shut your eyes while Mother sings
  Of wonderful sights that be,
And you shall see the beautiful things
  As you rock in the misty sea
  Where the old shoe rocked the fishermen three:—
      Wynken,
      Blynken,
      And Nod.

Wynken, Blynken, and Nod, by Eugene Field - Annotated

Wynken, Blynken, and Nod, by Eugene Field	Syllable Count
Wynken, Blynken, and Nod one night¬	8
Sailed off in a wooden shoe,—	7
Sailed on a river of crystal light	9
Into a sea of dew.	6
"Where are you going, and what do you wish?"	10
The old moon asked the three.	6
"We have come to fish for the herring-fish	10
That live in this beautiful sea;	8
Nets of silver and gold have we,"	8
Said Wynken,	3
Blynken,	2
And Nod.	2
The old moon laughed and sang a song,	8
As they rocked in the wooden shoe;	8
And the wind that sped them all night long	9
Ruffled the waves of dew;	6
The little stars were the herring-fish	9
That lived in the beautiful sea.	8
"Now cast your nets wherever you wish,—	9
Never afraid are we!"	6
So cried the stars to the fishermen three,	10
Wynken,	2
Blynken,	2
And Nod.	2
All night long their nets they threw	7
To the stars in the twinkling foam,—	9
Then down from the skies came the wooden shoe,	10
Bringing the fishermen home:	7
'Twas all so pretty a sail, it seemed	9
As if it could not be;	6
And some folk thought 'twas a dream they'd dreamed	9
Of sailing that beautiful sea;	8
But I shall name you the fishermen three:	10
Wynken,	2
Blynken,	2
And Nod.	2
Wynken and Blynken are two little eyes,	10
And Nod is a little head,	7
And the wooden shoe that sailed the skies	9
Is a wee one's trundle-bed;	7
So shut your eyes while Mother sings	8
Of wonderful sights that be,	7
And you shall see the beautiful things	9
As you rock in the misty sea	8
Where the old shoe rocked the fishermen three:—	10
Wynken,	2
Blynken,	2
And Nod.	2

[1] Wynken, Blynken and Nod is a simple poem with a sweet metaphorical story. Wynken, Blynken and Nod are three fishermen who fish for the stars from the wooden shoe they use as a boat. They sail off on a 'river of crystal light' (perhaps moonlight?) which takes them into a sea of dew (the night sky?). They chat to the moon about their intentions, and he sings them a song and rocks them in their boat. They fish for the stars, who talk to them and are happy to be caught in the three fishermen's nets. Then they come home again, 'down from the skies' and many people didn't believe in their tale and said it must be a dream. However, the poem's speaker names the fishermen as Wynken, Blynken and Nod. The final stanza explains the metaphor: 'Wynken and Blynken are two little eyes/and Nod is a little head' – this is a tale of a child's bedtime and sleep. The speaker tells the child to close its eyes and dream 'and you shall see the beautiful things/as you rock in the misty sea'. You could ask the children to pick out their favourite parts of this poem to read aloud and discuss – why have they chosen those parts? You could ask them to draw the three fishermen and their wooden boat, and annotate it with lines from the poem. You could ask them to take particularly descriptive lines and use them as the beginning of their own writing. Whatever you choose to do with this poem, it is a lovely one to share with the children.

[2] Eugene Field (1850-1895) was an American writer, poet and journalist. He seems to have had a happy life, which is reflected in the humorous and upbeat tone of his writing. He and his wife had eight children together, so it is no surprise that his poetry was written for children. In his lifetime, it was hugely successful, with some being set to music.

[3] The rhythm of this poem is fairly regular and the length of the lines is very similar throughout, with the exception of the refrain of 'Wynken, Blynken and Nod'. This regular rhythm helps the overall feel of the poem (more explicit in the final stanza) of it as a bedtime nursery rhyme, intended to send children off to sleep.

YEAR 4

Guy Fawkes

I feel sorry for Guy Fawkes.

Every year, we burn him.
Every year!

It's been four hundred years,
since he was caught
and rightly punished.
Four hundred times
he has been flung
with laughter
on the flames.

Hasn't he been punished enough by now?

Let's look, with honesty, at his crime:
he plotted to blow up the king.
I know that's very bad.
But he didn't actually complete
the task that he had planned!

Additionally, he was only one
of several men
who plotted.

Why, then, do we blame him?
Just him.

So next time you are grinning
at the bonfire and the sparklers,
just spare a thought for old Guy Fawkes.

Does he deserve another burning?

Guy Fawkes - Annotated

A free verse poem is, in some ways, the easiest type of poetry to write. A free verse poem is a poem that does not rhyme and does not have a regular rhythm.

Line no.	Guy Fawkes	Syllable Count[1]
1	I feel sorry for Guy Fawkes.	7
2	Every year,[2] we burn him.	6
3	[2] Every year!	3
4	It's been [2] four hundred years,	6
5	since he was caught	4
6	and rightly punished.	5
7	[2] Four hundred times	4
8	he has been flung[3]	4
9	[3] with laughter	3
10	on the flames.	3
11	Hasn't he been punished enough by now?[4]	10
12	Let's look, with honesty, at his crime:	9
13	he plotted to blow up the king.	8
14	I know that's very bad.[5]	6
15	But he didn't actually complete	9
16	the task that he had planned!	6
17	Additionally, he was only one	10
18	of several men	4
19	who plotted.	3
20	Why, then, do we blame [2] him?	6
21	Just [2] him.[6]	2
22	So next time you are grinning	7
23	at the bonfire and the sparklers,	8
24	just spare a thought for old Guy Fawkes.	8
25	Does he deserve another burning?[7]	9

[4] This rhetorical question is made more powerful by being on its own in this way – it's a stanza all on its own.

[5] This is a huge understatement! But it almost comes across as quite weary – as if to say, 'yeah, yeah, I know, whatever, it's bad, fine'. The speaker seems to have completely lost sympathy for the act of burning Guy Fawkes.

[6] This is the shortest line in the poem. Why do the children think this is? Perhaps it's because these two words, combined with the rhetorical question on the previous line, put a question into our minds as to why we punish JUST Guy Fawkes. If we're going to punish people with huge annual events, why just him? Why not other revolutionaries and tyrants throughout history? Can the children think of some other people who deserve to be remembered for their crimes? Can the children think of some other people who deserve to be celebrated for their successes with a special day of celebration?

[7] Similarly to line 11, this is a stanza all on its own. It makes the rhetorical question really stand out – particularly because it's the final line. This, combined with line 11 and the two line stanza of lines 20&21 (which also contains a rhetorical question), implies that the speaker is really asking the reader to consider these questions. This is a poem which isn't giving you the answers – it wants you to discuss and consider them. It's quite persuasive, but ultimately, things are left up to you, the reader, to decide.

[1] The syllable count of this poem is really interesting. The poem tells us that we should forgive Guy Fawkes because it's been so long since he plotted to commit his crime. The implication is that as time passes, it matters less and less and should make people less and less angry. If you look at the number of syllables in each line, the number gets smaller as you progress through each stanza. 9-8-6, for example, or 10-4-3. There are only two exceptions to this rule.

One exception is in the final four lines: 7-8-8-9. You could discuss with the children why they think this is. Perhaps it's because the speaker is implying that we are holding on to the resentment and anger of the past – perhaps (s)he feels like we are building towards another problem. Perhaps it's because the speaker is implying that we haven't yet let the issue of Guy Fawkes go.

[1 (continued)] The second exception is line six. It has one additional syllable. Why is this? You could talk to the children about it. Perhaps it's because the speaker is implying that Guy Fawkes punishment wasn't right? Perhaps it's because the speaker is implying that when he was punished, it would probably have been a while after the event, and that might have sparked a fresh wave of outrage at his deeds, when the details of his crime came to light. Perhaps it's because the speaker is asking us to ponder the notion of punishment for crime – Guy Fawkes' punishment was very severe.

[2] The repetition on these lines could show that the burning of Guy Fawkes is repetitive – perhaps the speaker is feeling like (s)he is 'over' it – it's just repetitive and boring now.

[3] The verb 'flung', followed by the phrase 'with laughter', implies that we are not really thinking about it when we are burning Guy Fawkes. 'Flung' is a careless word and the idea that people laugh as they do it is quite callous and cruel.

Memories

The breezes gently bustle in;
set leaves and branches tussling,
with sounds that unlock memory's door
to summers that have gone before.

The thwack of racquet hitting ball,
the slop of cream on strawberries, all
let my imagination soar
to summers that have gone before.

Those times, long gone, in memory's eye
are dreams where joy can never die.
I can't compare this, that's for sure,
to summers that have gone before.

Reject this time, this place, this life,
this cumulative woe and strife:
return me, please, how I implore,
to summers that have gone before.

Memories - Annotated

This poem is written in the form of a kryielle. This is a French form of poetry. The name comes from the 'kyrie', which is a part of many Christian church services (a short prayer which either begins with or consists of the words 'Lord, have mercy'). Kyrielles therefore, as you might expect, were often traditionally religious in subject. However, as with most forms of poetry, they have evolved over the years and can now have any subject. A kyrielle can have as many or as few stanzas as the poet decides.

Line no.	Rhyme scheme/ Refrain [1]			Syllable Count [2]
1	A		The breezes gently bustle in; [3]	8
2	A		set leaves and branches tussling, [4]	8
3	B		with sounds that unlock memory's door [5]	8
4	B	R	to summers that have gone before. [6]	8
5	C		The thwack [7] of racquet hitting ball,	8
6	C		the slop [7] of cream on strawberries, all	8
7	B		let [8] my imagination soar	8
8	B	R	to summers that have gone before.	8
9	D		Those times, long gone, in memory's eye	8
10	D		are dreams where joy can never die. [9]	8
11	B		I can't compare this, [10] that's for sure,	8
12	B	R	to summers that have gone before.	8
13	E		Reject this time, this place, this life, [11]	8
14	E		this cumulative [12] woe and strife:	8
15	B		return me, please, how I implore, [13]	8
16	B	R	to summers that have gone before.	8

[1] A kyrielle has a very specific rhyme scheme. As you see, each four-line stanza has an aabbR rhyme scheme. This means that lines one and two rhyme with one another and lines three and four rhyme with one another. The R means that line four is a refrain (a repeated section of a poem), which means that line four of each stanza is the same. In this case 'to summers that have gone before' is the refrain.

[2] A kyrielle is generally written (as this one is) in iambic tetrameter. This means that every line has eight syllables, broken down into four metrical feet consisting of two syllables each. A metrical foot in poetry is like a bar in music – it is how we separate rhythmic phrases of the same length. There are four metrical feet, called iambs, in each line of iambic tetrameter. Each iamb is a unit of rhythm which goes 'da-DUM'. Thus, a line of iambic tetrameter goes 'da-DUM da-DUM da-DUM da-DUM', where each 'da' and 'DUM' is one syllable. A word such as 'away' has a natural iambic rhythm, because we put the emphasis on the 'way' when we pronounce it, we wouldn't say 'A-way', we would say 'a-WAY'. If you emphasise the natural rhythm of speech when you read a kyrielle, you will notice the iambic rhythm immediately.

[3] The poem immediately begins by personifying the 'breezes' which 'bustle in'. But note that although the word 'bustle' seems fussy and perhaps a little bossy, they do so 'gently'. The speaker seems to be happy enough about being fussed in this way.

[4] 'Tussling' implies fighting, but in a gentle way, not a violent way. Again, it seems as though the speaker is being forced or coerced in some way to do something, but is not reluctant to do it.

[5] Here, we find that the sound of the leaves sparks a memory for the speaker. This helps us to make sense of the previous two lines – the sound of the breeze amongst the leaves has sparked a memory without the speaker's consent, as it were, but (s)he is not unhappy to be taken back to that memory, because it's a happy one. Again, there is personification on this line, of the sounds 'unlocking', as well as the metaphor of 'memory's door'.

[6] The refrain refers to what are clearly happy memories. You could argue that the noun 'summers' is a metaphor; perhaps it's just previous years that the speaker wants to return to, but in his/her memory they are 'summers' because they are warm, pleasant, happy memories.

[7] This onomatopoeia continues the aural imagery that has been created in the first stanza. Here we have additional sounds being added to create a fuller picture. Racquets and balls in the summer imply tennis, which is reinforced by the reference to strawberries and cream on the following line (the traditional tennis-watching snack - particularly at Wimbledon).

[8] The verb 'let' is fairly passive here – similarly to the first stanza, the speaker has been taken, almost involuntarily, back to the 'summers that have gone before'. There is nothing active or deliberate about it.

[9] This line is almost superlative in its description of the 'times, long gone' referred to on the previous line. There is a definite case of 'rose-tinted spectacles' going on – the 'summers that have gone before' are utterly perfect in this speaker's memory. Or, is this a comment on memory? The speaker could be saying that the way (s)he remembers these summers is so perfect, nothing can ever taint the 'joy' (s)he feels in remembering them.

[10] Suddenly, we have a hint of why the speaker is so bent on remembering the 'summers that have gone before'. What is 'this'? The phrase 'that's for sure', following the reference to whatever situation the speaker is currently in ('this') has a slightly bitter twist to it. We wonder what is so bad about 'this' that it is not even comparable to the previous sumemrs.

[11] The imperative verb 'reject' is a very strong one, here. This continues the negative feeling about the speaker's current situation, begun in the previous stanza, and amplifies it: the speaker is adamant that this 'time, this place' and even 'this life' must be rejected. The repetition of 'this' both on this line and the next and the pattern of three nouns on this line makes the rejection seems very strong. Perhaps even a tad melodramatic, but that's for you and the children to decide.

[12] This adjective implies that the speaker's life has been getting progressively worse – perhaps since those summers (s)he's been talking about.

[13] To whom is this line addressed? You could discuss this with the children. There is another imperative, like on line 13. Is this the speaker talking to the 'breezes' and asking them to return his/her mind to the memory of the 'summers that have gone before'?

Rosa Parks

The wonderfully brave Rosa Parks,
Said 'Wait! Why should I disembark
Or move down the bus?
Are you guys serious?'
And that's how she first made her mark.

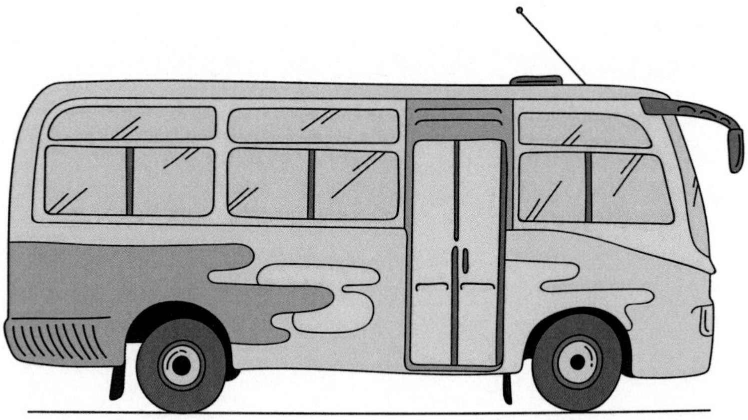

Rosa Parks - Annotated

The most common form of limerick is a five-line poem, usually written for humorous effect. The first, second and last lines rhyme with one another and are the same length as one another too. They are longer than the third and fourth lines, which are the same length as one another and rhyme with one another.

Line no.	Rhyme scheme	Rosa Parks [1]	Syllable Count
1	A	The wonderfully brave [2] Rosa Parks,	8
2	A	Said [3] 'Wait! [4] Why should I disembark	8
3	B	Or stand on the bus? [5]	5
4	B	Are you guys serious?' [5]	6
5	A	And that's how she first made her mark. [6]	8

[1] Rosa Parks (1913-2005) was an African American civil rights activist. She campaigned for civil rights in various different capacities for decades, but one of her most famous deeds was to refuse to give up her seat on a bus for a white man. Buses in most of the southern states of America during the 1950s were segregated. Rosa Parks boarded the bus after her shift at the department store in Montgomery where she worked and sat on one of the 'coloured' seats, as she legally had to. However, many bus drivers had adopted the unofficial policy of forcing black passengers to get up and give their seats to white passengers when the 'white' section was full. As Rosa Parks continued on her journey, the bus filled up and she was told to get up and move. She refused and was arrested. Martin Luther King, along with others in the civil rights movement, organised a city-wide boycott of the buses in reaction to Rosa's arrest (known as the Montgomery Bus Boycott). 500 people turned up to the courthouse to see her at her trial. Although she was fined, the boycott and its subsequent publicity were huge turning points in the civil rights movement.

[2] This description of Rosa Parks shows a very clear admiration for her on the part of the speaker.

[3] You will note that the speaker gives over more than half the poem to Rosa Parks' own voice. This shows respect and admiration for Rosa Parks on the part of the speaker.

[4] The imperative here shows the strength of character that the speaker wants to convey that Rosa Parks had.

[5] The rhetorical questions here both reinforce the strength of character the speaker shows Rosa Parks had and also encourage readers to engage with this issue and ask themselves these questions: why should she? How serious an issue was this? (Answer: very.) How serious an issue is it nowadays?

[6] The alliteration on this phrase highlights it as important: this was Rosa Parks making her first 'mark' on history. It could have been a tiny incident of the everyday institutional racism suffered by black people in America in the 1950s. Instead, it became a rallying point for the entire civil rights movement. That happened because she refused to move out of her seat! That was the beginning and that's how she first made her mark.

Freedom of Speech

1. Say it.
2. Question it.

3. Mention it.
4. Refer to it.

5. Voice it.
6. Talk it.

7. Declare it.
8. Pronounce it.

9. Answer it.
10. Exclaim it.

11. Shout it.
12. Reply to it.

13. State it.
14. Utter it.

15. Reveal it.
16. Tell it.

17. Express it.
18. Disclose it.

19. Whatever your 'it' is,
20. you have the right to speak it.

21. Whatever your 'it' is,
22. it is your 'it' to have.

23. Whatever your 'it' is,
24. address it to the nation.

25. Whatever your 'it' is,
26. pin it to the flag.

Freedom of Speech - Annotated

A list poem is exactly what it sounds like – a list. It can be a standard list of items, people or places. It can include lots of repetition or rhyme, but it doesn't have to. Usually a list poem will include some sort of comment on the list – its significance or what it means to the speaker – and might have a twist at the end.

Freedom of Speech	Syllable Count [1]
Say it. [2]	2
[2] Question it.	3
[2] Mention it.	3
[2] Refer to it.	4
[2] Voice it.	2
[2] Talk it.	2
[2] Declare it.	3
[2] Pronounce it.	3
[2] Answer it.	3
[2] Exclaim it.	3
[2] Shout it.	2
[2] Reply to it.	4
[2] State it.	2
[2] Utter it.	3
[2] Reveal it.	3
[2] Tell it.	2
[2] Express it.	3
[2] Disclose it.	3
Whatever your 'it' is, [3]	6
you have the right to speak it. [4]	7
[3] Whatever your 'it' is,	6
it is your 'it' to have. [5]	6
[3] Whatever your 'it' is,	6
address it to the nation. [6]	7
[3] Whatever your 'it' is,	6
pin it to the flag[6].	5

[1] The final 8 lines of this poem are the longest. They seem to balance out the poem, with a nice longer end to finish on, after a run of very short lines.

[2] Each of these lines consists of an imperative verb and a pronoun (with the occasional 'to' thrown in there). This is a loud poem – it is encouraging us to speak out lout – to use our voices to express ourselves. This reflects the title, because the poem is encouraging us to use our freedom of speech.

[3] What does this mean? Perhaps this is implying that everyone has something to say and whatever that is (the 'it' that is referred to) it's something we should be proud of and express (in the way the previous 18 lines have told us to!) Using the inverted commas in this way makes the word 'it' seem as if it stands out somehow. This makes it the focus of the line. This could be the speaker trying to say that whatever your 'it' is SHOULD be your focus and it should be shared.

[4] This is literally true. With some (few) exceptions, we, in this country, have the right to freedom of speech. The personal pronoun makes this feel like a direct address – I, as the reader, have this right. It's very blunt and up front; exactly as it's encouraging the reader to be.

[5] Having ownership over your own thoughts may not be a new idea, but it's an important one and this poem is encouraging its readers to take that ownership, by its use of personal pronouns.

[6] The use of 'nation' and 'flag' here seems to be referring again to our rights, given to us by the country we live in. In this country, we have freedom of speech and that's a legal right in society. These two nouns seem to be referring to that.

Light and Dark

The sun beams down brightly from the sky overhead,
so gorgeous in orangey-yellow and red,
as, smiling round greenly in the gentle breeze,
the trees stand up proudly and rustle their leaves.

In the light, sunny park, the glad children play,
yelling and laughing to friends all the way.
Noisy and bright, the daytime flies past
in a riot of colour we all wish would last.

Creepingly slow, sneaky night edges in
and elbows the daylight aside with a grin.
Bringing its blackness and painting the sky
with darkness the stars just can't break, though they try.

Silvering hedges and houses and heads,
the moon ages everything on which it treads.
Out come the nocturnal animals keenly
to feast and to play, while we all sleep dreamily.

Like a see-saw, the light and the dark swap their hold
on the earth, in a dance which is older than old.

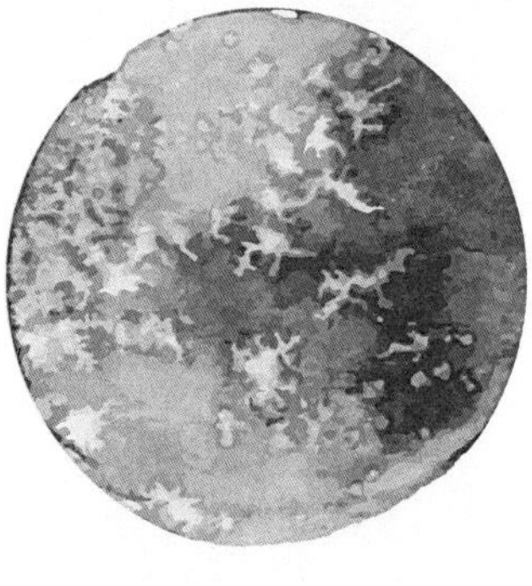

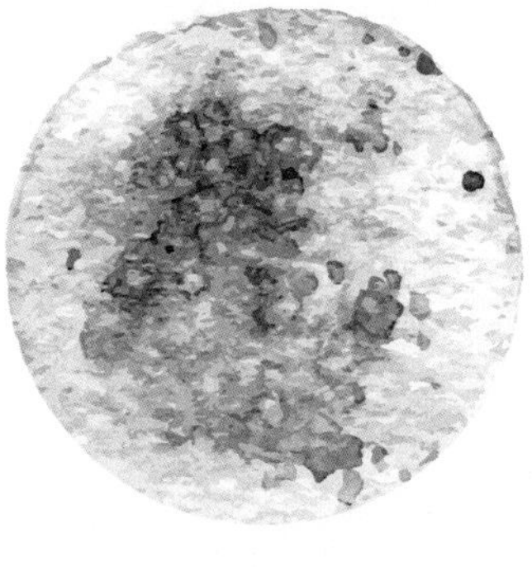

Light and Dark - Annotated

Line no.	Rhyme scheme	Light and Dark	Syllable Count
1	A	The sun beams [1] down brightly from the sky overhead,	12
2	A	so gorgeous in orangey-yellow [2] and red [2],	11
3	B	as, smiling [1] round greenly [2] in the gentle breeze,	11
4	B	the trees stand up proudly [1] and rustle their leaves.	11
5	C	In the light, sunny park, the glad children play,	11
6	C	yelling and laughing to friends all the way.	10
7	D	Noisy and bright, the daytime flies [1] past	9
8	D	in a riot of colour [2] we all wish would last.	12
9	E	[3] Creepingly slow, sneaky [3] night edges in [1]	10
10	E	[1,3] and elbows the daylight [2] aside with a grin,	11
11	F	bringing its blackness and painting [2] the sky [1]	10
12	F	with darkness [2] the stars just can't break, though they try. [1]	11
13	G	Silvering [2] hedges and houses and heads, [4]	10
14	G	the moon ages everything on which it treads. [1]	11
15	H	Out come the nocturnal animals keenly [1]	11
16	H	to feast and to play, while we all sleep dreamily.	12
17	I	Like a see-saw, the light and the dark [2] swap their hold [1]	12
18	I	on the earth, in a dance [1] which is older than old. [5]	12

[5] Why is this 'dance' 'older than old'? What do the children think this could mean? It could be because the 'dance' dates back to the very origins of the Earth, so 'old' is not enough. It could be a more obscure metaphor – perhaps for good and evil or happiness and sadness. The metaphor of the dance is quite a pleasant one – the light and the dark are in some way partners. Linking this with the simile from the previous line of 'like a see-saw', there are connotations here of balance.

[1] These are examples of personification. Throughout the poem, several inanimate objects are given human qualities – that's what makes a personification poem! Alternatively, you can choose one specific thing to personify throughout your poem. A few examples of objects that are personified in this poem are: the night, the stars, the sun and animals. This is generally done by choosing a verb which relates to a specifically human action (or an adverb which describes a way of doing something that is specifically human) and applying it to something which is not human.

[2] There are lots of references to colour in this poem. They combine to create a very visual image of the scenery the poem describes. Combining the colour imagery with the personification makes the poem seem more appealing to the reader, because we are not only able to picture it very clearly, but we can also feel the emotion the personified objects are feeling in their turn. Perhaps you could ask the children to spot all the colours or references to visual imagery in the poem. Perhaps they could draw the scenes from the poem, using the colours.

[3] The personality given to the night here is quite comical. Perhaps the children could write a story or draw a picture showing the sneaky night grinning! Why do they think the speaker has chosen to call the night 'sneaky'? What is 'sneaky' about the night? Perhaps it's because it comes quite slowly. Perhaps it's because it lurks around the other side of the world and then pounces on us. Perhaps it's because when it's dark it's easier to 'get away' with things.

[4] The alliteration here could be likened to the sound of a sigh – 'hhhhhh' – why might the speaker have chosen to create a 'sighing' sound here? Perhaps because it's dark now, so the speaker is slowing down and feeling tired. Perhaps because the moon is making him/her feel old (as in the following line, where the moon 'ages everything on which it treads').

The Romans

They marched in strict formation
right across the nation
to bring us education
and build us irrigation,
the Romans, when they came.

They marched with banners flying
to bring us baths to lie in,
cures to stop us dying
and laws to stop us defying,
the Romans, when they came.

They marched through many lands and
brought benefits they'd planned and
caused trouble they'd expand and
entirely misunderstand,
the Romans, when they came.

However much they charmed us,
they still enslaved and harmed us.
Finally, they disarmed us,
which thoroughly alarmed us:
the Romans, when they left.

The Romans - Annotated

Line no.	Rhyme scheme		Syllable Count[1]
1	A	They marched[2] in strict formation	7
2	A	right across the nation	6
3	A	to bring us education[3]	7
4	A	and build us irrigation[3],	7
5	B R	the Romans, when they came.[4]	6
6	C	They marched[2] with banners flying	7
7	C	to bring us baths to lie in[3],	7
8	C	cures[3] to stop us dying	6
9	C	and laws[3] to stop us defying,	8
10	B R	the Romans, when they came.	6
11	D	They marched[2] through many lands and	7
12	D	brought benefits they'd planned and	7
13	D	caused trouble they'd expand and	7
14	D	entirely misunderstand,[5]	7
15	B R	the Romans, when they came.	6
16	E	However much they charmed us,	7
17	E	they still enslaved and harmed us.	7
18	E	Finally, they disarmed us,[6]	7
19	E	which thoroughly alarmed us:	7
20	F R	the Romans, when they left.[7]	6

[4] This refrain acts as a marker for the end of each stanza. You could compare it to a flag or a gap between battalions of the army as they march.

[5] The verb 'misunderstand' is interesting here because it's quite a kind one. The Romans are not portrayed as terrible tyrants who caused trouble for the sake of it. Instead, they have come to conquer the country because they, perhaps, haven't understood the wants and needs of the native people. The story of Pocahontas would be an interesting parallel here.

[6] There is a deliberate ambiguity here, where the speaker could be talking about taking away weapons, but actually, if you look at the next two lines and what happens (i.e. the Romans leaving) it could be meant in more of a 'disarmed=won over' sense.

[7] The change in this final refrain is quite sudden. Having just that final word be different on this line is quite shocking, in a way, and could leave the reader feeling fairly bereft – which is probably the feeling the speaker was intending to go for. The Romans were interlopers, but when they left it was difficult for the country to re-adjust. Perhaps that is the feeling the speaker wants to communicate.

[1] You will notice that the syllable count is very regular in this poem, as is the rhyme scheme. There is also a refrain which repeats at the end of each stanza. It would appear that the speaker has deliberately kept this poem as regular and rhythmic as possible in order to reflect the organized and regulated nature of the Roman army – the 'strict formation' mentioned on the first line.

[2] Using the pronoun 'they' is quite a vague way of referring to the Romans. Although we know who 'they' are before the first line because of the title, it still makes the poem seem more menacing, in a way, because there's a vague, nameless 'they' which has 'marched' across the land. There is a militaristic feel to the verb 'marched' as well – we can work out that they are probably soldiers from this verb, which makes them seem scarier.

[3] These are just some of the benefits brought to England and other countries by the Romans. There is an interesting comparison though between these benefits and the way they're talked about – the form of the poem seems to emphasise how scary it must have been to have soldiers taking over your country (with the strong, marching rhythm and the constant repetition of 'the Romans, when they came' and 'they marched'). In comparison to this, the benefits that are mentioned are definitely good things, on the whole – until we reach the final one: laws to stop us defying is interesting. It could be good, because having a lawful society if a good thing, but it could also be bad, because it's about stopping us defying the Romans (who are the ones taking over our country!) so that could be negative. You could ask the children to research the benefits the Romans brought to England and make a list. And/or you could ask them to imagine how it must have felt to have soldiers roaming through the countryside and taking over – they began to decide what was best for the native tribes and tell them what to do. How would that feel?

Friendships (An acrostic)

Friendships can be made in moments,
Rooted in a wink or smile.
In a heartbeat, bonds are formed:
Elastic that can stretch a mile.
No-one's heart survives alone, all
Dwellers on this planet know.
Sharing life with friends is how our
Happiness will build and grow.
In a friendship, things will change.
People grow apart sometimes.
Somehow, though, the bond remains.

Friendships (An acrostic) - Annotated

Line no.[1]	Rhyme scheme[1]	Friendships (An acrostic)[2]	Syllable Count[3]
1	A	Friendships can be made in moments,[4]	8
2	B	Rooted in a wink or smile.[5]	7
3	C	In a heartbeat,[6] bonds are formed:	7
4	B	Elastic that can stretch a mile.[7]	8
5	D	No-one's heart survives alone, all	8
6	E	Dwellers on this planet know.	7
7	F	Sharing life with friends is how our	8
8	E	Happiness will build and grow.[8]	7
9	G	In a friendship, things will change.	7
10	H	People grow apart sometimes.	7
11	G	Somehow, though, the bond remains.[9]	7

[1] The number of lines in this poem, as well as the rhyme scheme, create an interesting effect at the end of the poem. The final three lines state that friendships change – these three lines are where the poem changes also, from an ABCB rhyme scheme to an ABA rhyme scheme. You could separate this poem into three stanzas, if you so wished, of four lines, four lines and then the final three lines. This is interesting, because although the final three lines are still in the same rhythm and still have a similar rhyme, they are subtly different. This could be said to be reflective of the changes the poem says happen within friendships.

[2] An acrostic is a poem in which the first letter of every line spells a word or sentence. In this case: FRIENDSHIPS

[3] The rhythm of this poem is very regular. There are either 7 or 8 syllables on each line. This could be said to reflect a 'good' friendship – it can be counted on to remain steady. Not unchanging, but regular and solid.

[4] The alliteration here makes this 'moment' seem a bit more special. This could be implying that the moments in which friendships are made are special. You could discuss this concept with the children: do they agree that friendships can be made in moments? Do they think it takes longer?

[5] The metaphor on the word 'rooted' implies that friendships are like plants or trees – they grow and develop and blossom. Perhaps you could ask the children to draw a 'friendship tree'. Can they think of any other metaphors that would work as well or even better? They could also look deeper into this metaphor. In what way could a friendship be said to be 'rooted in a wink or smile'? What does a wink or smile mean in this metaphor – soil? Water?

[6] In addition to the idea of 'in a heartbeat' being a small amount of time, there is also the implication that friendships affect your heart and maybe even get your heart to 'skip a beat' in the way we say for other relationships.

[7] The implication of this metaphor of 'elastic' is that it doesn't matter how far apart friends are, they will still care for each other.

[8] The verbs 'build' and 'grow' link back to line 2 and the idea of friendships being like a plant.

[9] This phrase links back to the word 'bond' on line 3, implying that the bonds of friendship are everlasting, no matter what happens.

Choices.
More every day.
How do I choose safely?
Where can I turn for clear guidance?
Help me.

Choices - Annotated

Line no.	Choices	Syllable Count[1]
1	Choices.[2]	2
2	More every day.[3]	4
3	How do I choose safely?[4]	6
4	Where can I turn for clear guidance?[5]	8
5	Help me.[6]	2

[1] This poem is a cinquain (pronounced sin-cane). This means that the lines follow a strict syllable pattern. The pattern of syllables shown here (2, 4, 6, 8, 2) is the one we follow for the cinquains in this book. There are other types of cinquains which use different numbers of syllables on their five lines. However, we have chosen to follow this structure. Cinquains can have more than one stanza, each of which follows the same syllabic structure.

[2] This first line uses a full stop to make the reader stop and consider this word. Choices. This links to the moral aspect of SMSC. Morality is about making choices and as children grow up they are faced with more and more choices (as the second line of the poem says). You could discuss with the children what choices they have to make today...tomorrow... next year.

[3] This line refers to the children growing up and facing more choices and challenges. The structure of the poem reflects this growth as well – each line grows and develops, until the final one. Why do the children think that final line is so short? Is it because it is separate to the rest of the poem? Is it because it represents a backwards step in the person's life, where they need to ask for help? Is it because this is where the poem changes and becomes a direct address to the reader (with the imperative verb and personal pronoun)?

[4] Again, as with the first line, where we are left with one word and a full stop, making us ponder the meaning of that one word, here the speaker has used a technique to make us think and consider. In this case, (s)he has used a rhetorical question. Another important point to note is that we are left at the end of the line with the adverb 'safely'. This is the important part of the line – it's not about just choosing, but choosing 'safely'. Choosing correctly. This can seem overwhelming for children. This would be a good conversation starter about how we know what are safe choices. How do we keep ourselves safe?

[5] Another rhetorical question – the reader is really expected to think about this poem! This is directing the reader to consider where (s)he could get help from an outside source. This would be a good opportunity to discuss organisations that could provide support for your children if they need it. The school, local GP surgery, Childline, the NSPCC, Action for Children, etc. This line uses the noun 'guidance' – this is not about the children doing something that they are anxious about. It's just about them having someone to talk to and discuss their worries and concerns, however big or small.

[6] This imperative, plus the personal pronoun, makes this a very personal line, which appeals directly to the reader. This could be an opportunity for the children to discuss what advice they could offer a friend in a scenario you devise for them (or they devise for themselves). They could even use the poem in a role-play or script, taking the lines and expanding on them.

The Volcano

Belching
clouds
of steam,

the stone giant squats
on the landscape obnoxiously.
A carpet of trees, a reluctant throne,
shrug aside, sullenly, irritably, unwillingly.

Ever watchful water waits – a prison of dreams and missed opportunities.

The Volcano - Annotated

This is an image poem. Image poems are really good ones to encourage the children to write, because you can be as supportive or as flexible as you feel the children need you to be and there is a simple start point for them to begin collating ideas. In brief, the children use a high quality image and write about it. However, they can use it in the sense of a very vague startpoint – 'tell me what this makes you think of' – or you can create a really specific set of criteria about the image – 'pick five features that you can see within the poem and use word association to come up with ten words which relate to each one...etc.' The poem can be super short or as long as the children (and/or you) want it to be. The idea of an image poem is to make children think really hard about their word choice. Does that adjective fully describe the real 'blueness' of the water? Does that verb fully portray the massive strength of the bird, if it should choose to move?

Line no.	The Volcano	Syllable Count[1]
1	Belching[2]	2
2	clouds	1
3	of steam,	2
4	the stone giant[2] squats[2]	5
5	on the landscape obnoxiously[2].	8
6	A carpet of trees, a reluctant throne,	10
7	shrug[2] aside, sullenly[2], irritably[2], unwillingly.[2,3]	14
8	Ever watchful[2] water waits[2,4] – a prison of dreams and missed opportunities.[5]	19

[1] The layout of this poem reflects the image, because it looks like the volcano and the lake. The lines get steadily longer and longer. Do the children find this effective? Why/why not?

[2] There is a lot of personification in this poem. Perhaps the children could spot all the personification words and assign them to the parts of the image they refer to. They could even come up with some more personification words and write their own poem or paragraph creating personification. Can they describe the personalities of the three things that are personified (the volcano, the trees and the water), based on the words used in the poem? Perhaps they could write a conversation between two of the personified objects?

[3] The pattern of three adverbs here gives an interesting 'personality' to the personification of the trees. There is a clash between the volcano and the trees. Perhaps the children could consider the differences between stone and trees – living vs. not living, growing and changing vs. fixed and unchanging etc.

[4] The alliteration here gives an interesting effect to this phrase – it seems to slow it down as you say it (like a tongue twister) and emphasises the 'waiting' that the water is doing. Why is it watchful? What is it waiting for? You could ask the children to speculate. Could it be that it's waiting for the volcano to erupt? Could that be why the trees have reluctantly made room for the volcano – because it is so threatening? Could it be that the water is waiting for the volcano and the trees to be washed away? In terms of age, the trees are very young compared to the volcano, but the volcano is very young compared to the ageless water, which used to cover everything and perhaps is waiting for an opportunity to cover everything again.

[5] What makes the water a metaphorical 'prison'? Is it keeping the volcano in check by acting as a barrier to stop the lava, if the volcano were ever to erupt? Is it stopping the growth of the trees expanding beyond its borders? Is it both? Why would it be keeping anything in a prison? What are the 'dreams and missed opportunities' that are mentioned? What dreams might a volcano have? You could discuss these questions with the children.

The Ballad of Elizabeth Fry

Elizabeth Fry (1780-1845) was a pioneering campaigner for better conditions in prisons during the Victorian Period.

Now hear the tale I sing to you,
Of love and noble toil.
A story of Elizabeth;
A credit to England's soil.

Born in the east of our fair isle,
She grew up as a Quaker.
How could she know, that little girl
Just where her life would take her?

A child of twelve, her mother died,
Poor Lizzy took the lead,
In bringing up her siblings –
A strong young girl indeed.

Six years went by, Elizabeth
Met William Savery,
Who opened up her eyes to
Prejudice and bigotry.

Elizabeth was heartbroken
To think of people's plight.
The poor, the needy, prisoners
Who were not treated right.

Her head went up, her heels dug in,
She stood, strong, firm and tall,
Refusing to accept that justice
Couldn't be had by all.

Aged twenty, she was married
To a chap named Joseph Fry.
With their eleven children
They were more than satisfied.

But she still sensed so strongly
That she had a special job
Only she could see was needed:
Her voice could move the mob.

In 1812 this feeling
Really overwhelmed her mind
When she visited a prison
Where conditions were a crime.

In tiny cells, filthy and damp,
The desperate folk were piled.
Starving, feeble skeletons,
Most died before their trial.

Fry's kind and gentle manner
Now was put up to the test.
As she struggled for acceptance
In a world where men knew best.

This strong, courageous woman
Fought for what she knew was right
And in 1818, finally
She brought her cause to light.

At a House of Commons meeting,
She explained the prisoners' plight.
The government could not ignore
What she forced into their sight.

For years she campaigned tirelessly
And caused some huge reforms.
Never before had women been
So important to England's laws.

Her argument for human rights
Was way before its time.
She tried to show that convicts
Needed help, despite their crime.

With simple love and kindness,
Elizabeth inspired.
Generations of young women
Found their imaginations fired.

Not only Queen Victoria
(Who was an avid fan)
But even Florence Nightingale:
Fry showed that women can

Take charge and have opinions
And can change things if they try.
So it's with thanks, we end the ballad
Of the unique Mrs. Fry.

The Ballad of Elizabeth Fry - Annotated

A ballad is a poem which tells a story. It is usually a love story, but not always. Ballads date back thousands of years and, in their earliest forms, were usually designed to be sung. For this reason, they have a fairly regular rhythm and a very regular rhyme scheme. The rhyme scheme is usually abXb, where X is a choice: it can rhyme with 'a' or it can not. Ballads are usually composed of four-line stanzas.

Line no.	Rhyme scheme	The Ballad of Elizabeth Fry *Elizabeth Fry (1780-1845) was a pioneering campaigner for better conditions in prisons during the Victorian Period.*	Syllable Count[1]
1	A	Now hear the tale I sing to you,[2]	8
2	B	Of love[3] and noble toil.	6
3	C	A story of Elizabeth;	8
4	B	A credit to England's soil.	7
5	D	Born in the east of our fair isle,[4]	8
6	E	She grew up as a Quaker.[5]	7
7	F	How could she know, that little girl[6]	8
8	E	Just where her life would take her?	7
9	G	A child of twelve, her mother died,	8
10	H	Poor Lizzy[7] took the lead,	6
11	I	In bringing up her siblings –	7
12	H	A strong young girl[7] indeed.	6
13	J	Six years went by, Elizabeth	8
14	K	Met William Savery,[8]	6
15	L	Who opened up her eyes to	7
16	K	Prejudice and bigotry.	7
17	M	Elizabeth was heartbroken	8
18	N	To think of people's plight.	6
19	O	The poor, the needy, prisoners	8
20	N	Who were not treated right.	6
21	P	Her head went up, her heels dug in,[9]	8
22	Q	[9] She stood, strong, firm and tall,	6
23	R	Refusing to accept that justice	9
24	Q	Couldn't be had by all.	6
25	S	Aged twenty, she was married	7
26	T	To a chap named Joseph Fry.	7
27	U	With their eleven children	7
28	T	They were more than satisfied.	7
29	V	But she still sensed so strongly[10]	7
30	W	That she had a special job	7
31	X	Only she could see was needed:	8
32	W	Her voice could move the mob.	6
33	Y	In 1812 this feeling	7
34	Z	Really overwhelmed her mind	7
35	AA	When she visited a prison	8
36	Z	Where conditions were a crime.[11]	7
37	BB	In tiny cells, filthy and damp,[12]	8
38	CC	[12] The desperate folk were piled.	6
39	DD	[12] Starving, feeble skeletons,	7
40	CC	Most died before their trial.[13]	6
41	EE	Fry's kind and gentle manner	7
42	FF	Now was put up to the test.	7
43	GG	As she struggled for acceptance	8

[1] The rhythm is fairly regular, to fit the song-like or chant-like ethos of the poem, so you can see that the number of syllables on each line are generally very similar. One thing you could do with the children is spot any particularly long or short lines and consider why they might be so short/long. Is there a particularly important message that needed to be given in that line?

[2] Using the verb 'sing' here is important, as ballads are often sung, so this fits nicely with the poetic form.

[3] The noun 'love' here is important too, because a ballad is usually a love song. This is not exactly a love song, as it not written by someone who is in love with Elizabeth Fry. However, it's about the love she showed for others, so the speaker has deliberately used this noun early in the poem to show the importance of love in the poem.

[4] Using the personal pronoun 'our', combined with the adjective 'fair' makes this a very inclusive sentence – it's not 'her' country, or 'your country', it's 'ours'. It sets up a pride in our country and we automatically feel glad to be a part of the same country as Elizabeth Fry.

[5] In case the children don't know, Quakers are a Christian group who believe that there is a part of God in everyone. Quakers believe in peace and equality. These beliefs may have influenced Elizabeth Fry in her work.

[6] Calling her a 'little girl', especially with the adjective 'little', makes us feel a bit sorry and sympathetic towards Elizabeth Fry. This brings us closer into her story and makes us want to read on and find out what is going to happen to her.

[7] In the space of three lines, the speaker calls Elizabeth 'poor Lizzy' and 'a strong young girl'. Could this reflect how quickly the little girl needed to grow up to become a mother to her small siblings?

[8] William Savery was an American Quaker who worked to help people who were being persecuted in the late eighteenth and early nineteenth centuries, specifically Native Americans and slaves. He travelled to Europe in 1796 and met Elizabeth Fry two years later in February 1798.

[9] These three metaphors use Elizabeth's physical behaviour to represent her mental preparation for the task ahead of her.

[10] The alliteration on this line (or, strictly speaking, sibilance – repetition of 's' sounds) creates an aural effect which reinforces the verb 'sensed' on this line. It sounds like whispers, which links to the idea of 'sensing' something.

The Ballad of Elizabeth Fry - Annotated

Line no.	Rhyme scheme	The Ballad of Elizabeth Fry *Elizabeth Fry (1780-1845) was a pioneering campaigner for better conditions in prisons during the Victorian Period.*	Syllable Count [1]
44	FF	In a world where men knew best. [14]	7
45	HH	This strong, courageous woman	7
46	II	Fought for what she knew was right	7
47	JJ	And in 1818, finally	9
48	II	She brought her cause to light.	6
49	KK	At a House of Commons meeting,	8
50	LL	She explained the prisoners' plight.	7
51	MM	The government could not ignore	8
52	LL	What she forced into their sight.	7
53	NN	For years she campaigned tirelessly	8
54	OO	And caused some huge reforms.	6
55	PP	Never before had women been	8
56	OO	So important to England's laws.	8
57	QQ	Her argument for human rights	8
58	RR	Was way before its time.	6
59	SS	She tried to show that convicts	7
60	RR	Needed help, despite their crime.	7
61	TT	With simple love and kindness, [15]	7
62	UU	Elizabeth inspired.	6
63	VV	Generations of young women	8
64	UU	Found their imaginations fired.	8
65	WW	Not only Queen Victoria	8
66	XX	(Who was an avid fan)	6
67	YY	But even Florence Nightingale:	8
68	XX	Fry showed that women can	6
69	ZZ	Take charge and have opinions	7
70	AAA	And can change things if they try.	7
71	BBB	So it's with thanks, we end the ballad	9
72	AAA	Of the unique Mrs. Fry.	7

[11] This metaphor is ironic, because it uses the noun 'crime' to talk about not the things the prisoners had done to be put in prison, but the way they were treated when they were in there.

[12] The adjectives used on these lines combine to create a terrible picture of the conditions the prisoners had to suffer. Using so many adjectives builds up the picture and creates sympathy for the prisoners.

[13] This is a very blunt statement, which, following the descriptive lines in the rest of the stanza, seems harsher for its shortness.

[14] This is an interesting line to draw out to the children. What does the speaker mean? The past tense implies that this was a situation which is no longer the case. Do the children agree that men know best? Do woman know best? Are we all equal? What must it have been like for Elizabeth Fry in a time when women's opinions didn't matter? Perhaps explain to them that the suffragettes (who fought and died for women's rights – particularly the right to vote) only succeeded in getting women the vote over 100 years after Elizabeth Fry appeared in the House of Commons.

[15] The adjective 'simple' could be said to be a reference to Elizabeth Fry's Quaker beliefs, as Quakers believe in keeping their lives simple and pure. This is also another reference to love, which is what the poem began with discussing.

'Hope' is the thing with feathers-
That perches in the soul-
And sings the tune without the words-
And never stops-at all-

And sweetest-in the Gale-is heard-
And sore must be the storm-
That could abash the little Bird
That kept so many warm-

I've heard it in the chillest land-
And on the strangest Sea-
Yet, never, in Extremity,
It asked a crumb-of Me.

'Hope' is the thing with feathers, Emily Dickinson - Annotated YEAR 4

Line no.	Rhyme scheme[1]	'Hope' is the thing with feathers, Emily Dickinson[2]	Syllable Count[3]
1	A	'Hope' is the thing with feathers[4] —[5]	7
2	B	That perches[4] in the soul—	6
3	C	And sings[4] the tune without the words[6]—[5]	8
4	B	And never stops—[5] at all—	6
5	D	And sweetest—[5] in the Gale[7]—[5] is heard—[5]	8
6	E	And sore must be the storm[7,8]—[5]	6
7	D	That could abash the little Bird[4]	8
8	E	That kept so many warm —[5]	6
9	F	I've heard it in the chillest[9] land—[5]	8
10	G	And on the strangest Sea[10]—[5]	6
11	G	Yet, never, in Extremity,	8
12	G	It asked a crumb—[5] of Me.	6

[1] There is a fairly regular rhyme scheme in this poem. Lines 3 and 11 don't fit into the pattern though. Perhaps you could ask the children why they think this is. It could be because there is something special about those lines, or it could be because Dickinson is hinting that life is irregular – there are little bumps in the road – but hope carries you over the bumps.

[2] Emily Dickinson (1830-1855) was an American poet. She wrote almost 1800 poems during her life but published hardly any. A lot of her poetry focuses on the beauty of the world around her – the magic of the everyday miracle.

[3] Most of Dickinson's poetry is written in 'ballad stanza', which is composed of quatrains (four line sections) of alternating iambic tetrameter and trimeter. This means that, as you can see, the odd numbered lines have eight syllables and the even numbered lines have six. You can then further break the lines down into metrical feet. A metrical foot in poetry is like a bar in music – it is how we separate rhythmic phrases of the same length. There are four metrical feet (called iambs) in tetrameter and three in trimeter. Each iamb is a unit of rhythm which goes 'da-DUM'. Thus, a line of iambic pentameter goes 'da-DUM da-DUM da-DUM da-DUM da-DUM', where each 'da' and 'DUM' is one syllable. A word such as 'away' has a natural iambic rhythm, because we put the emphasis on the 'way' when we pronounce it, we wouldn't say 'A-way', we would say 'a-WAY'. If you emphasise the natural rhythm of speech when you read a poem composed in iambic meter, you will notice the iambic rhythm immediately. This may be too complex for the children to understand, but it's useful for you to know and you can introduce them to the idea of rhythm, stanzas and potentially different types of rhythm.

[4] The metaphor on line one (repeated in the title) links the abstract concept of 'hope' to a bird. This metaphor is then extended throughout the poem. You could ask the children to play a word association game with the word 'bird'. What does it make them think of? Perhaps it's something wild and free. Perhaps it's something sweet and beautiful. Either way, it seems that Dickinson's point here is that hope is a desirable quality, which brings happiness to a person's life without asking anything in return.

[5] Dickinson often breaks up her poems with dashes in this manner. The rhythm is so swiftly flowing that she uses the dashes to emphasise certain words or ideas. Perhaps you could ask the children to look at the dashes and suggest why they think the dashes are put in the positions Dickinson has chosen.

[6] What could this phrase mean? There is alliteration here, which highlights this phrase and could mean that it's important. Why would this 'little Bird' sing 'without the words'? Is this a hint at the idea that hope doesn't necessarily rely on logic and calmly thought out arguments, but on emotion?

[7] The weather imagery on these lines creates a new metaphor in which the wind/storm represents a difficult situation in someone's life.

[8] The alliteration here links the words 'sore' and 'storm' together. You could point out to the children that it's not just the 's' that is repeated, it's the 'or' digraph too. This makes the words link together even more closely. This line is Dickinson saying that the situation would have to be extremely dire (a very 'sore' 'storm') for the 'little Bird' of hope to be 'abashed' or defeated. Hope springs eternal.

[9] You're right. This isn't a real word. It's poetic license! You could discuss this with the children. How far can you stretch poetic license before your writing becomes incomprehensible? Should you? Why/why not?

[10] The alliteration here could reflect the 'swooshing' sound of the sea, or perhaps the sound of the bird's wings flapping.

There is one that has a head without an eye,
And there's one that has an eye without a head.
You may find the answer if you try;
And when all is said,
Half the answer hangs upon a thread.

A Riddle, by Christina Rossetti - Annotated

Line no.	Rhyme scheme	A Riddle,[1] by Christina Rossetti[2]	Syllable Count
1	A	There is one that has a head without an eye,[3]	11
2	B	And there's one that has an eye without a head.[3]	11
3	A	You[4] may find the answer if you[4] try;	9
4	B	And when all is said,	5
5	B	Half the answer hangs upon a thread.[5]	9

[1] A riddle asks the listener to work out the answer to a cleverly phrased question or to work out what a cleverly phrased statement is referring to. They are usually light-hearted and fun. You could ask the children if they can work out the answer to this riddle! (It's pins and needles, by the way. Or, rather, a pin and a needle. A pin has a head, but no eye. A needle has an eye, but no head. Half the answer – the needle – hangs upon a thread. Literally.)

[2] Christina Rossetti (5 December 1830 – 29 December 1894) was an English poet. She wrote a large number of poems, often romantic and/or religious, and she wrote several poems for children. Rossetti's father was Italian and her mother was English. She grew up in London, publishing her first poems aged 18. Her siblings were also artists. One of her brothers, Dante Gabriel Rossetti, was an artist and poet. Her other brother, William, and her sister, Maria, were both writers. Christina Rossetti's most famous poems are Goblin Market and In the Bleak Midwinter (which was later set to music by Gustav Holst and is now a famous Christmas carol).

[3] The juxtaposition of these identical sentence structures, with the reversal of the two main nouns (eye and head) is typical of a riddle. This is the sort of word play you can expect from this type of poem. These two lines are more or less identical, but contrast one of the parts of the answer to the other part.

[4] Speaking directly to the reader in this way, using personal pronouns, helps the poem become more personal. It feels as if the writer is talking directly to us.

[5] This phrase seems metaphorical, because the implication could be that the answer is tenuous and brittle and hanging just out of reach of the person who is trying to solve the riddle. However, this is also actually literal – a needle does hang upon a thread.

Love's Philosophy, by Percy Bysshe Shelley

The fountains mingle with the river
And the rivers with the ocean,
The winds of heaven mix for ever
With a sweet emotion;
Nothing in the world is single;
All things by a law divine
In one spirit meet and mingle.
Why not I with thine?—

See the mountains kiss high heaven
And the waves clasp one another;
No sister-flower would be forgiven
If it disdained its brother;
And the sunlight clasps the earth
And the moonbeams kiss the sea:
What is all this sweet work worth
If thou kiss not me?

Love's Philosophy, by Percy Bysshe Shelley - Annotated YEAR 4

Line no.	Rhyme scheme	Love's Philosophy, by Percy Bysshe Shelley[1]	Syllable Count
1	A	The fountains[2] mingle[3] with the river[2]	9
2	B	And the rivers[2] with the ocean[2],	8
3	A	The winds of heaven mix[3] for ever	9
4	B	With a sweet emotion;	6
5	C	Nothing in the world is single;	8
6	D	All things by a law divine	7
7	C	In one spirit meet and mingle[3].	8
8	D	Why not I with thine?—[4]	5
9	E	See the mountains kiss[3] high heaven	8
10	F	And the waves clasp[3] one another;	8
11	E	No sister-flower would be forgiven	10
12	F	If it disdained its brother;	7
13	G	And the sunlight[5] clasps[3] the earth	7
14	H	And the moonbeams[5] kiss[3] the sea:	7
15	G	What is all this sweet work[6] worth	7
16	H	[4]If thou kiss[3] not me?	5

[1] Percy Bysshe Shelley, (1792-1822), was an English poet and writer. He was married twice, the second time to Mary Shelley (the author of Frankenstein) and had several children. Shelley was a very progressive person in his day. He was an atheist who promoted non-violence and whose strong beliefs around morality and politics influenced activists such as Karl Marx and Mahatma Gandhi. His poetry is extremely influential. Shelley was a strong advocate of the beauty and divinity of nature in his poetry. This can be seen in this poem as he links the love between himself and the person he is writing to (and addresses on lines 8 and 16 directly) to natural images.

[2] The different types of water here are going from smallest to largest. Is that significant? You could discuss that with the children. Does it represent the emotions the couple have been through – love beginning, then growing and expanding into an 'ocean' of emotion? Also, they go from least to most natural. It begins in a manmade construction – a fountain (perhaps representing where the couple met; in society), continues into a river (which could go through towns and cities, but is less contained) and ends in an ocean (completely wild and untamed).

[3] There are several verbs throughout the poem which refer to combining two things. This is a linking thread which keeps the images of the poem connected to one another. They are also personifying the aspects of nature that the speaker is discussing, as the verbs used as 'human' verbs.

[4] Lines 8 and 16 are the only two in which the speaker directly addresses the reader. This poem appears to be written to the speaker's lover; (s)he seems to be appealing to him/her to 'kiss' him and possibly to marry him/her. The personal pronouns are archaic 'thine' and 'thou'. However, it might be worth pointing out to the children that 'thou' used to used in an informal situation, thereby implying that the speaker feels that (s)he has a close relationship with the person (s)he is addressing. 'Thou' was used to address members of your family, close friends (who were social equals) and partners. Additionally, these are the two shortest lines in the poem. Why do the children think that is? Is it to make them stand out? The poem has a fairly regular rhythm, so these two lines are very much stand-alone. Perhaps this represents the speaker giving a romantic speech, then stopping to whisper in his/her lover's ear or speak more directly, with less flowery language.

[5] This juxtaposition of day and night implies the universality of the feelings and actions that the speaker is discussing. (S)he is implying that it's natural and normal to be in love and to allow that love to follow its logical progression and end in kissing/marriage.

[6] What 'sweet work' is the speaker discussing? Is it the 'work' of courtship? Or the 'work' (s)he's had in writing the poem to appeal to his/her lover?

Had I the heavens' embroidered cloths,
Enwrought with golden and silver light,
The blue and the dim and the dark cloths
Of night and light and the half light,
I would spread the cloths under your feet:
But I, being poor, have only my dreams;
I have spread my dreams under your feet;
Tread softly because you tread on my dreams.

He wishes for the cloths of heaven - Annotated

Line no.	Rhyme scheme[1]	He wishes for the cloths of heaven,[2] by W. B. Yeats[3]	Syllable Count[4]
1	A	Had I the heavens' embroidered[5] cloths,	9
2	B	Enwrought with golden and silver[6] light,	9
3	A	The blue and the dim and the dark cloths[7]	9
4	B	Of night and light and the half light,	8
5	C	I would spread the cloths under your feet:	9
6	D	But I, being poor,[8] have only my dreams;	10
7	C	I have spread my dreams under your feet;	9
8	D	Tread softly[9] because you tread on my dreams.	10

[1] Strictly speaking, there is no rhyme at the end of the lines of this poem. The 'rhyme' is achieved by repetition of the key words: cloths, light, feet and dreams. There is some internal rhyme, however ('night and light and the half-light'), and other repeated words within the lines, such as 'tread' and 'spread', all of which makes the poem seem comforting or familiar in some way. The constant repetition brings those words home in a way that couldn't be achieved any other way.

[2] In this poem, the 'cloths of heaven' can be taken to be a metaphor relating to the skies. The speaker is saying that if (s)he had the skies – if they were his/hers to own – (s)he would spread them under the feet of his/her lover. This can be said to be reminiscent of Walter Raleigh's spreading his cloak under the feet of Queen Elizabeth I, reflective of gallantry and humility.

[3] William Butler Yeats (1865-1939) was an extremely influential Irish poet. He was the first Irishman to win the Nobel Prize in Literature. Yeats' poetry is largely lyrical, naturalistic and spiritual.

[4] The rhythm of this poem is very regular. There is little variation between the length of the lines. Note also that the poem is one long sentence. There is no end punctuation on any of the lines – it's all colons and semi-colons. This seems to be a short speech to the speaker's lover, which the speaker has left no room in for the lover to reply. Why could that be? Perhaps it's a declaration of love as a build up to a marriage proposal? Perhaps it could even be representative of marriage vows.

[5] What do the children think the metaphorical verb 'embroidered' means in this context? What images are 'embroidered' onto the skies? Perhaps stars, clouds, the moon, the sun, etc.

[6] This appears to be a metaphorical reference to night and day.

[7] A lovely activity based on this poem could be to draw the 'cloths of heaven'. This repetitive line creates images of the different colours of the sky at different times of day. Linking this to the previous line's reference to day and night, this could be a hint that the love the speaker feels for the person (s)he wrote the poem for is eternal and will last through periods of darkness.

[8] Would the children agree that we automatically feel sympathy for the speaker when we learn that (s)he is poor? What effect do they think that creates?

[9] Why do we need to tread softly on dreams? Are they fragile and easily broken? Or is it this person's dreams in particular which are fragile? Why could that be? Why has the speaker spread his/her 'dreams' under this person's feet – what is the significance of this? These are all questions you could ask the children to think about.

YEAR 5

Florence Nightingale

It's said that Florence Nightingale,
liked to slide down the staircase rail,
to give her patients help and care.
Would it not have been safer to take the stair?

A clerihew is a four line poem about a famous person. Every clerihew should begin with the name of the famous person the poem is about as the first line. It can be the whole line, or just most of the line. The rhyme scheme is always AABB and the rhythm is usually fairly regular, but it doesn't have to be. The clerihew ought to gently poke fun at the famous person, in a funny, but not unkind, way. Often a reference to the reason that they're famous is included.

Line no.	Florence Nightingale
1	It's said that Florence Nightingale,[1]
2	liked to slide down the staircase rail,[2]
3	to give her patients help and care.[3]
4	Would it not have been safer to take the stair?[4]

[1] 'It's said' implies that it's a rumour – this is perhaps a fun way of poking fun at the clerihew itself. Rumours are not to be trusted and neither is the information in this poem!

[2] There is a bit of sibilance here in 'slide' and 'staircase'. This adds to the silliness and makes the poem flow.

[3] Here, we have the reference to what Florence Nightingale was actually famous for, as most Clerihews have. The fact that the speaker has said 'help and care' as opposed to 'medical treatment', shows that the speaker thinks of Florence Nightingale as a caring and kind individual – this might be an acknowledgement that although the speaker is being silly and making fun of her, (s)he still has respect for her.

[4] A rhetorical question. The rhythm is created by a slightly odd word order, but it still is perfectly understandable. The reference to 'safer' is another acknowledgement that Florence Nightingale was a nurse, so she was making the hospital safer for people – and perhaps she ought to have been safe herself!

Elizabeth I

If I were a queen,
the first Elizabeth would
be my role model.

A Tudor princess,
they all said she should marry,
but she ruled alone.

A long reign of peace
was the last thing expected.
What an achievement!

Elizabeth I - Annotated

A haiku is a traditional Japanese poem, based on a specific number of syllables per line. The first and third lines have five syllables and the second line has seven. Sometimes poets write haiku chains, i.e. a series of haikus on the same or related subjects.

Line no.	Elizabeth I	Syllable Count
1	If I were a queen,[1]	5
2	the first Elizabeth[2] would	7
3	be my role model.	5
4	A Tudor princess,[3]	5
5	they all said[4] she should marry,	7
6	but she ruled alone.	5
7	A long reign of peace	5
8	was the last thing expected.[5]	7
9	What an achievement![6]	5

[1] The first line of this poem is the kind of wish/dream that many little girls have. The only difference is that quite often little girls want to be princesses, not queens. A queen is a more responsible job. You could discuss this with the children – what's the effect of the speaker wanting to be a 'queen' instead of a 'princess'?

[2] Why has the speaker chosen to say 'the first Elizabeth' rather than 'Elizabeth the First'? It's an odd sentence construction. Perhaps the speaker has chosen to position 'the first' at the beginning to show that Elizabeth I is 'first' in his/her opinion.

[3] The use of 'princess' here, where previously it was 'queen' is interesting – it positions Elizabeth as a weaker person, making the last line of this haiku 'but she ruled alone' much stronger – she was young when she came to power and she was barely even a 'princess' in many people's eyes, but she managed to bring peace and prosperity to the land and she did it 'alone'.

[4] Who is 'they all'? This could be a reference to the lords and ladies of the court, the people of England...or is it a reference to men in general? It could be showing how strong she was in a patriarchal society.

[5] This is an interesting phrase, simply because you could ask the children – why? Why did nobody expect a long reign of peace? Was it because the Tudors were notoriously difficult and warmongering? Or was it because she was a woman?

[6] This exclamation at the end shows the depth of admiration the speaker has for Elizabeth I. Leaving this as the final thought encourages the reader to agree with the speaker.

The Digestive System

To be a survivor, you must have saliva:
that's where your digestion begins.

Your teeth are the chewers, squish squashy pursuers
of every edible thing.

Your tongue is a pusher, a flexible smoosher
moving food to your throat, as you know.

Then down your oesophagus, right from the topagus
down to the bottom it goes.

Now the stomach takes charge, with an acidic sparge
and, slowly, it kick-starts digestion.

Then the smaller intestine, curled up tight like a question
mark offers its enzyme suggestions.

From little to large, next intestine takes charge
to finish the process at last.

Then whatever is left (by now well past its best)
can be – let's say 'got rid of', or 'passed'.

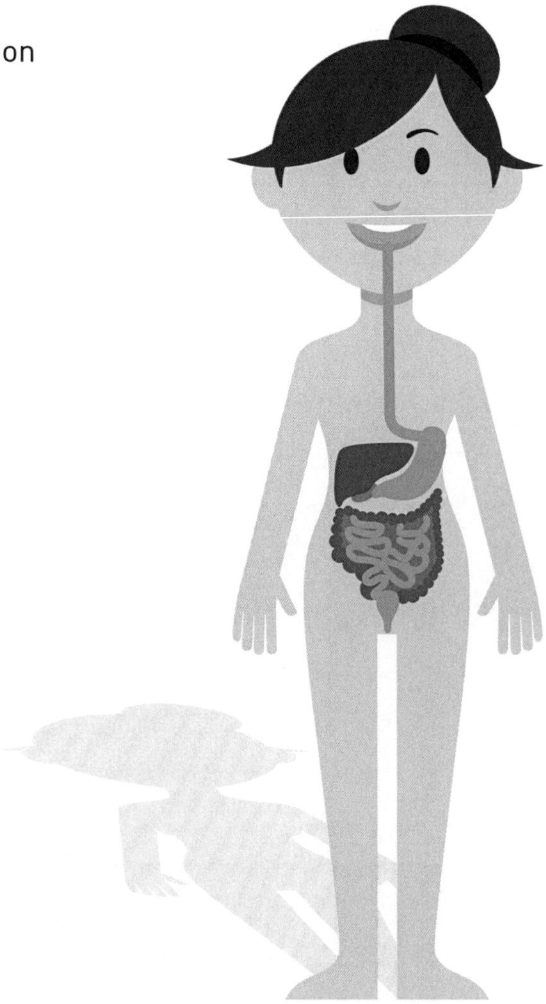

The Digestive System - Annotated

A list poem is exactly what it sounds like – a list. It can be a standard list of items, people or places. It can include lots of repetition or rhyme, but it doesn't have to. Usually a list poem will include some sort of comment on the list – its significance or what it means to the speaker – and might have a twist at the end.

Line no.	Rhyme scheme	The Digestive System	Syllable Count
1	A	To be a survivor,[1] you must have saliva:[2]	12
2	B	that's where your food's journey[3] begins.	8
3	C	Your teeth are the chewers, squish squashy[4] pursuers	12
4	B	of every[5] edible thing.	8
5	D	Your tongue is a pusher, a flexible smoosher	12
6	E	moving food to your throat, as you know.[6]	9
7	F	Then down your oesophagus, right from the topagus[7]	13
8	E	down to the bottom it goes.	7
9	G	Now the stomach takes charge,[8] with an acidic sparge	12
10	H	and, slowly, it kick-starts digestion.	9
11	I	Then the smaller intestine, curled up like a question	13
12	H	mark offers its enzyme suggestions.	9
13	J	From little to large, next intestine takes charge	11
14	K	to finish the process at last.	8
15	L	Then whatever is left (by now well past its best)[9]	12
16	K	can be – let's say 'got rid of', or 'passed'.[10]	9

[1] Literally – if you are to survive, you have to eat. To eat, you need saliva.

[2] The internal rhyme on this line (internal rhyme is where a word within a line rhymes with another word within or at the end of the line) is mirrored on every other line of the poem (the odd numbered ones). You could discuss the effect of this with the children. Why hasn't the writer put each rhyming section on a new line? What effect would it have if the poem was set out differently?

[3] This refers back to the title of the poem. The metaphor of 'journey' and the personification of 'food' here makes what could possibly be seen as a slightly distasteful topic (forgive the terrible pun!) a bit lighter and more personal. There is also a sense of comedy created here, by the combination of the internal rhyme, the steady rhythm and the personification of the food.

[4] This nonsense phrase refers to the actions of the teeth. Its nonsensical nature adds to the comedy and keeps the tone light.

[5] To fit in with the rhythm, this word needs to be said in a slightly unnatural way, emphasizing every syllable individually: ev-er-y. This is both a type of poetic license and also adds to the comic feel of the poem more generally. This technique is repeated on lines 5 and 7.

[6] Addressing this comment directly to the reader, along with the use of personal pronouns throughout the poem, makes the poem much more personal and stops it from being like a lecture on the digestive system – it's like a close conversation between the speaker and reader instead.

[7] The way this is described makes it seem almost like a slide; something enjoyable. This contributes to the personification begun in the title of the poem. The repetition of 'down' on this line and the following one, in addition to the nonsense word 'topagus', is what creates this feeling.

[8] More personification here, of the stomach. The whole process is made more like a journey by the personification not only of the food, but also other things throughout the poem. This relates to lines 3, 5, 9, 12 and 13 as well.

[9] The brackets here add to the comic tone of the poem. Using the phrase 'past its best' is amusing because it's almost euphemistic in its under-stating of the case.

[10] More euphemisms! It might be fun and interesting to discuss with the children why going to the toilet is such a taboo subject. We tend to consider it something quite disgusting, but it's a completely natural process. Perhaps the speaker (by using so many euphemisms) is hinting at this.

Tolerance

It's a timely smile, that says "I know
that's what you choose to do".
It's a friendly hand, that says "OK,
that's what you're born to be".

It's an open mind, that embraces
all of nature's bounty.
It's a trusting heart, that welcomes in
anybody's choices.

It's the strength of spirit
to recognise the struggle it can be
to merely function in the world
when all the space is taken up with 'us', but you're a 'them'.
It's putting all those crass assumptions
in a small balloon, then letting go
and watching, gladly, as they fly away.

The breeze that softly blows them away
comes from a place of love
and of acceptance. That's tolerance:
when 'us' means 'everyone'.

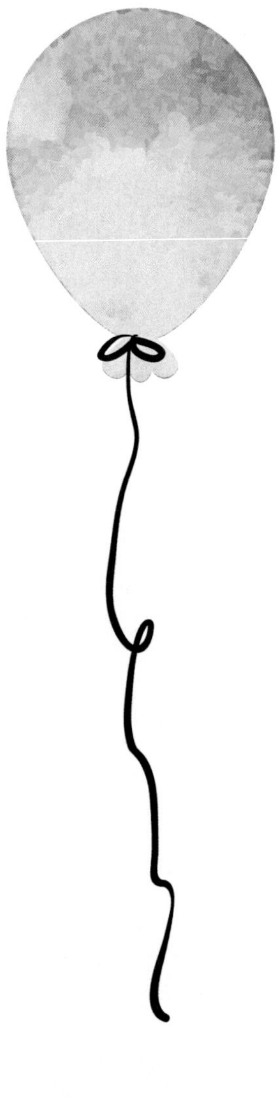

Tolerance - Annotated

A metaphor poem uses an extended metaphor (which runs throughout the poem) or a series of metaphors, usually to describe one thing or explain one idea.

Notice the regularity of the rhythm in this poem. There are alternate lines of 9, then 6 syllables each. From line 9 to line 15, this rhythm is broken. Perhaps this is to show what it's like to feel 'different' to people around you. Perhaps this is to show that 'different' isn't always a bad thing. Perhaps it is to show that intolerance breaks the natural rhythms of life. You could discuss this with the children.

Line no.	Tolerance	Syllable Count
1	It's a timely smile,[1] that says[2] "I know	9
2	that's what you choose to do".[3]	6
3	It's a friendly hand,[4] that says "OK,	9
4	[3] that's what you're born to be".	6
5	It's an open mind,[5] that embraces	9
6	all of nature's bounty.[6]	6
7	It's a trusting heart,[7] that welcomes in	9
8	[6] anybody's choices.	6
9	It's the strength of spirit[8]	6
10	[8] to recognise the struggle it can be	10
11	to merely function[9] in the world	8
12	when all the space is taken up with 'us', but you're a 'them'.[10]	14
13	It's putting all those crass assumptions[11]	9
14	in a small balloon,[12] then letting go	9
15	and watching, gladly, as they fly off.	9
16	The breeze that softly blows them away[13]	9
17	comes from a place of love	6
18	and of acceptance. That's tolerance:	9
19	when 'us' means 'everyone'.[14]	6

[1] This first metaphor links back to the title – we know that the speaker is talking about tolerance. The adjective here is interesting – why is it a 'timely' smile? Perhaps you could discuss with the children what 'times' tolerance might/should be shown.

[2] Not only is this line a metaphor – here it becomes personification too! The smile is what is 'saying' something here.

[3] The juxtaposition of these two lines shows how tolerance means accepting people both for their choices and for what's innate in them.

[4] A second metaphor; what is the hand doing – it could be helping someone up, it could be shaking their hand, it could be stopping someone from being unkind to someone else. You could discuss the power of gesture with the children.

[5] A third metaphor, which is almost a cliché – why has the speaker chosen to use it? Perhaps because although it's quite overused, in juxtaposition with the previous two metaphors and the one following metaphor, it makes up 'smile', 'hand', 'mind' and 'heart' – a series of images which build up to describe a person and how a person relates to another.

[6] The juxtaposition of these two lines is similar to the juxtaposition of lines 2 and 4. Again, there is the link made between choices and nature – the point perhaps being that tolerance refers both to what people do and who they are.

[7] Metaphor 4 – this is an interesting one. 'Trusting' is an odd choice of adjective. Why does a tolerant person have to be trusting? Perhaps because we have to trust that people can make the right decisions for themselves. Perhaps because we should give people the benefit of the doubt, rather than judging them based on appearances or a choice they have made. You could discuss this with the children.

[8] The sibilance here emphasizes the 's' words. This juxtaposes strength and struggle, showing that the speaker feels respect for those people who are struggling to find tolerance in their lives.

[9] The adverb 'merely' emphasizes the difficulties some people face.

[10] Who is this 'us'? Who is this 'them'? The speaker seems to be trying to encapsulate the sense of isolation people feel when they are 'different' for any reason. Using the personal pronoun 'you're' makes this seem very personal to the reader, so it encourages empathy with those who feel this sense of isolation.

[11] Whose? Is this a reference to your own 'crass assumptions' and therefore allowing yourself to be a better person by removing them? Or is it referring to other people's assumptions and just letting go and not allowing them to drag you down with them? You could discuss this with the children.

[12] Perhaps the adjective 'small' here is implying that people who judge and are intolerant are 'small'.

[13] This metaphor for removing someone's intolerant views is interesting. It is a very gentle image. Where the speaker could have been nasty to/about intolerant people or intolerant views, instead (s)he has chosen to be quite calm and non-judgemental. The adverb 'softly' shows us this.

[14] This is a really nice summary of the poem's message. The previous line ending with a colon both separates and joins this line to the rest of the poem. It is joined by the enjambment, but it is separated by the pause caused by the colon. This is an effective way to show that this is related to the poem, but that it stands on its own too - it is a summary of what the poem has been saying.

Light Lines

If I didn't have you,
I wouldn't think to wonder
Why the sun doesn't have light-lines
Stretching all the way to yonder.

I wouldn't search the trees and
Try to you-ify the reason
Why we draw our suns with these on
Regardless of the season.

If I didn't have you,
I would never hear described
How the beard that cover Santa's mouth
Could maybe reach his eyes.

I wouldn't sit, in stifled glee
As you rest on the big man's knee
Describing how his eyes would see
Out from the whiteness, fuzzily.

If I didn't have you,
My mind wouldn't invent
What would happen if a monster
Went and camped out in a bin-tent.

I wouldn't scratch my head
And try to think of how a bed
Could be made out of things you said
Would be found in the bin by Fred (the monster).

If I didn't have you,
I would take things as they come.
I'd never question, dream or wonder,
If I'd never been your mum.

And of nothing am I surer
Than that life would be much poorer
Without being the adorer
Of my wonderful explorer.

Light Lines - Annotated

There is an unusual rhyme scheme in this poem. The stanzas alternate between an ABCB rhyme and an AAAA rhyme. You could discuss this with the children and ask them why they think the speaker has done it like that. Is it to make it more like a conversation; as if the speaker is addressing the person to whom this poem is written? Is it for comic effect? Is it to show the difference between the speaker and the child?

Line no.	Rhyme scheme		Syllable Count
1	A	If I didn't have you,[1]	6
2	B	I wouldn't think to wonder	7
3	C	Why the sun doesn't have light lines[2]	8
4	B	Stretching all the way to yonder.	8
5	D	I wouldn't search the trees and	7
6	D	Try to you-ify[3] the reason	8
7	D	Why we draw our suns with these on[4]	8
8	D	Regardless of the season.	7
9	E	If I didn't have you,[5]	6
10	F	I would never hear described	7
11	G	How the beard that covers Santa's mouth	9
12	F	Could maybe reach his eyes.	6
13	H	I wouldn't sit, in stifled glee[6]	8
14	H	As you rest on the big man's knee	8
15	H	Describing how his eyes would see	8
16	H	Out from the whiteness, fuzzily.	8
17	I	If I didn't have you,	6
18	J	My mind wouldn't invent	6
19	K	What would happen if a monster	8
20	J	Went and camped out in a bin-tent.[7]	8
21	L	I wouldn't scratch my head	6
22	L	And try to think of how a bed	8
23	L	Could be made out of things you said	8
24	(L)	Would be found in the bin by Fred (the monster).[8]	8 (11)
25	M	If I didn't have you,	6
26	N	I would take things as they come.	7
27	O	I'd never question, dream or wonder,[9]	9
28	N	If I'd never been your mum.	7
29	P	And of nothing am I surer	8
30	P	Than that life would be much poorer	8
31	P	Without being the adorer[10]	
32	P	Of my wonderful explorer.[11]	8

[1] Immediately, we have two characters set up in this poem: 'I' and 'you'. Initially, we might wonder who these people are. It is not made explicit until the penultimate stanza that the speaker is the mother and she is speaking to her child. However, there are hints throughout the poem and it appears clearer and clearer as the poem continues, until the explicit 'If I'd never been your mum' on line 28. The poem is therefore in some respects building towards the 'reveal' of the final two stanzas.

[2] Here, we have a reference to the title of the poem. Literally, when this line is taken with line 7, we can assume that the 'light-lines' referred to are those we draw in a 'basic' portrayal of the sun, such as we would draw for or with a young child. Additionally, however, if we look at the title of the poem, we can perhaps glean from it that the poet sees this as a useful metaphor for her relationship with her child – perhaps because the child 'lights up' her life or because they're connected by an invisible 'umbilical cord' of light and love. You could discuss this with the children.

[3] This nonsense word could be said to add to the moderately comic tone of the poem. It is also quite an awkward word, perhaps reflecting the awkwardness of the conversation or the explanation that this mother has come up with in response to her child's question.

[4] You could discuss with the children why we do draw suns with lines coming out of them. You could discuss 'visual metaphor' and what the lines represent.

[5] The repetition of this line at the beginning of every second stanza draws a linking line throughout the poem. The speaker doesn't really seem to be imagining her life without her child, as there is no sadness to the poem's tone. Instead, it is an ode to how rich the speaker's life has been made by her child.

[6] This short phrase is important, because up until this point of the poem, there is no specific reference made to the mother's feelings about these events. There is a lightness to it and a comic feel, caused by the nonsense words and phrases like 'wouldn't think to wonder' and 'search the trees', which implies that she isn't cross about them and is putting lots of thought into the converstions, despite how apparently 'silly' they are, but she never explicitly says that she's enjoying them until this line.

[7] More nonsense! In this instance it's a compound word, which helps us to understand what it means: 'a tent made out of a bin'. This is an amusing image, as well as a nonsense word, which adds to the comic effect.

[8] This is an odd line. The speaker has added this information in in brackets – almost as if she's saying it in an aside to the reader. This adds to the feeling throughout the poem that this is a poem to be said aloud – it is representing a conversation (or perhaps a speech). This technique extends the line, but the brackets make it clear that the last two lines are not entirely a part of the line. It's where the speaker almost breaks out of poetry and into conversation/prose.

[9] This pattern of three is lovely, because it really shows the power of the speaker's imagination when inspired by her child.

[10] This is the only noun that refers directly to the speaker. She describes herself as the 'adorer' of her child. Using this verb as a noun transforms it from being something that could be transitory (i.e. 'I adore you' – this describes this specific moment in time and something that could change) to something permanent. This speaker cannot change what she is – she is the adorer.

[11] Again, the child has never really been described properly in the poem. His/her actions and questions have been described, but not the child him/herself. This is a very short but very meaningful part of the poem. The adjective 'wonderful' is deliberately ambiguous – as well as the standard meaning of the word as 'great', it also means 'inspires wonder' and 'is full of wonder'. Each of these meanings works. Additionally, the word 'explorer' is a lovely way to describe this curious child. You could discuss with the children what this implies.

The Earth

Soothingly familiar, but never the same,
she cradles us all in her arms.
With infinite wisdom and love without end,
her rainbow smiles beam through the day.
At night, with compassion, she gazes with care
from a million twinkling eyes
to watch over us as we sleep away stress –
feeling comforted, knowing she's there.
She feeds us, she clothes us, she's all that we need.
She's generous still to a fault,
despite all the scars that we've left on her face,
despite all the tears she has wept.
Despite the disease of destruction we've caused
and the burning tattoos we have left
through forests and rivers and steep mountainsides,
she's still taking care of us now.
So the question I ask and the worry I have
is this: who will take care of her?

The Earth - Annotated

The rhythm of this poem is loosely dactylic. A dactyl is a metrical foot consisting of one stressed and two unstressed syllables (DUM-da-da). An example of a word which contains a natural dactylic rhythm is 'infinite' A metrical foot in poetry is like a bar in music – it is how we separate rhythmic phrases of the same length. Although the rhythm of this poem is not a strict dactylic meter, it has approximately four dactyls on every odd-numbered line and three on each even-numbered line. It's very musical and very consistent. This could reflect the constancy of the world – how it is 'soothingly familiar' and how it spins perfectly in space, ever to the same rhythm and motion.

Line no.		Syllable Count
1	Soothingly familiar, but never the same,[1]	11
2	she cradles us all in her arms.[2]	8
3	With infinite[3] wisdom and love without end,	11
4	her rainbow smiles[4] beam through the day.	8
5	At night, with compassion, she gazes with care	11
6	from a million twinkling eyes[5]	9
7	to watch over us as we sleep away stress[6] –	11
8	feeling comforted, knowing she's there.	9
9	She feeds us, she clothes us, she's all that we need.[7]	11
10	She's generous still to a fault,[8]	8
11	despite[9] all the scars that we've left on her face,	11
12	despite[9] all the tears she has wept.	8
13	Despite9 the disease of destruction[10] we've caused	11
14	and the burning tattoos[11] we have left	9
15	through forests and rivers and steep mountainsides,	11
16	she's still taking care of us now.	8
17	So the question I ask and the worry I have[12]	12
18	is this: who will take care of her?	8

[1] The juxtaposition of these contrasting images creates a comparison. The world is familiar, inasmuch as we know its cycles and our small part of it. However, it never remains the same – it is eternally changing, both in terms of culture, physical landscape and the fact that it moves.

[2] Who is 'she'? This is the first piece of personification. The Earth is 'she' – could this be a reference to 'Mother Earth'? Perhaps it's a coincidence that the speaker has chosen to use the female pronoun.

[3] This adjective is sneakily ambiguous. There is the colloquial meaning of 'infinite', i.e. plenty of! There is also the literal meaning – we are talking about the Earth and therefore, potentially, the origins of the universe, which some would claim is infinite in every respect – time and space.

[4] A clever little metaphor which refers not only to the shape of a rainbow as like the shape of a smile (albeit upside down) but also that a rainbow carries connotations of happiness and peace.

[5] The implication here is that the Earth is watching over us through the stars – the stars are her eyes.

[6] The sibilance here is relaxing and paints an aural picture of sleep, quiet and calm.

[7] It is literally true that we get everything we need from the Earth. However, the personification in the verbs 'feeds' and 'clothes' makes the Earth seem generous and kind – like a mother.

[8] This is the first hint of anything that might be negative – the word 'fault' is ambiguous because there is the potential to read it as a 'fault-line' – there is therefore a bit of a sinister twist to this line.

[9] The repetition here is powerful. Occurring at the beginning of three consecutive lines, the word 'despite' reinforces the negative turn this poem has taken and turns it around on the reader by using the personal and inclusive pronoun 'we' on each of these lines to denote the destruction we, as a species, have caused on the Earth.

[10] The alliteration is quite harsh here. The repetition of the plosive 'd' reflects the negative and brutal tone which the speaker has just adopted.

[11] This noun is an interesting use of personification – a tattoo is a very human thing to have, but giving a tattoo against someone's will is also a very abusive thing to do.

[12] Previous to this, this poem has been much more inclusive than this. The only personal pronoun used has been 'we', but now it's 'I'. It's as though the speaker is removing him/herself from the 'we' and is now being mildy accusing to the reader. Using the repetitive grammar structure wherein the speaker has said both 'question I ask' and also 'worry I have' does soften it slightly, because a question can be accusing, but a worry cannot really. However, there is a definite expectation that although this is a rhetorical question (therefore not requiring an answer) the speaker still wants the reader to really think about this and come up with a solution.

Holding your hand

When you were born, I felt the world stand still.
The sun, for wonder, paused his graceful dance.
All living creatures held their breath until
I held your tiny hand and with one glance
I knew you. Then and there, I promised you,
that I would be a better person. But
such promises are really hard to do,
when real life encroaches. We're not shut
away from irritations in the world.
Reality won't let us be alone.
Alone: where time is crystallised like pearl
and we are back together and I'm home.
I can but hope that you will understand
how hard I've tried to keep holding your hand.

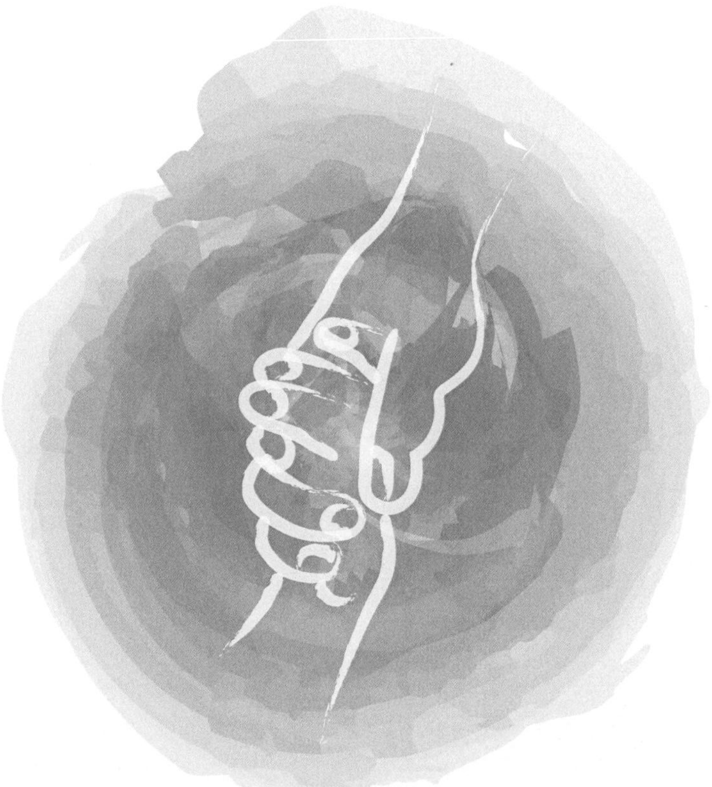

Holding your hand - Annotated

Originally, sonnets came from Italy and gradually evolved to mean a fourteen line poem with a regular rhyme scheme and rhythm. When sonnets first came to England, they were written in the Italian style; a style known as Petrarchan. Later, English poets, including Shakespeare, adopted and adapted the sonnet form into the most usual form known today, which is (perhaps unfairly, as Shakespeare did not invent it) known as the Shakespearean sonnet. Sonnets have a very specific rhythm and rhyme scheme. They are usually about love.

A Shakespearean sonnet has an ABAB rhyme scheme throughout, until the final two lines, which are a rhyming couplet.

A Shakespearean sonnet is written in iambic pentameter. This means that every line has ten syllables, broken down into five metrical feet consisting of two syllables each. A metrical foot in poetry is like a bar in music – it is how we separate rhythmic phrases of the same length. There are five metrical feet, called iambs, in each line of iambic pentameter. Each iamb is a unit of rhythm which goes 'da-DUM'. Thus, a line of iambic pentameter goes 'da-DUM da-DUM da-DUM da-DUM da-DUM', where each 'da' and 'DUM' is one syllable. A word such as 'away' has a natural iambic rhythm, because we put the emphasis on the 'way' when we pronounce it, we wouldn't say 'A-way', we would say 'a-WAY'. If you emphasise the natural rhythm of speech when you read a sonnet, you will notice the iambic rhythm immediately.

Line no.	Rhyme scheme	Sonnet	Syllable Count
1	A	When you were born,[1] I felt the world stand still.[2]	10
2	B	The sun, for wonder, paused his graceful dance.[3]	10
3	A	All living creatures held their breath[4] until	10
4	B	I held your tiny hand[5] and with one glance	10
5	C	I *knew* you.[6] Then and there, I promised you,	10
6	D	that I would be a better person.[7] But[8]	10
7	C	such promises are really hard to do,[9]	10
8	D	when real life encroaches. We're not shut	10
9	E	away from irritations in the world.[10]	10
10	F	Reality won't let us be alone.[11]	10
11	E	Alone:[12] where time is crystallised like pearl[13]	10
12	F	and we are back together and I'm home.[14]	10
13	G	I can but hope that you will understand	10
14	G	how hard I've tried to keep holding your hand.[15]	10

[1] A sonnet is usually a love poem between adult partners. This poem immediately makes itself different, as it is clear that the speaker is addressing a child.

[2] This metaphor is the opposite to the one usually used as a cliché in adult relationships – 'the earth moved'. This image of standing still and wanting the world to pause is a powerful one – the implication is that the speaker was so happy in that moment, that (s) he didn't want it to ever end.

[3] The personification on this line shows the speaker demonstrating the strength of the emotion (s)he felt on the birth of the child. Even the sun is affected. The sun could be a metaphor for the most important thing in his/her life up till then, or even for his/her life.

[4] Another metaphor which shows the significance of this event to the speaker. (S)he is implying that every living creature did what (s)he presumably did – held their breath.

[5] The personal pronoun 'your' makes this poem feel really 'close to home', as if the speaker is speaking directly to the reader. The adjective 'tiny' reinforces the image of the baby and shows a protectiveness on the part of the speaker, reinforced by the idea that the speaker is holding the baby's hand.

[6] The word 'knew' is the only one in the poem which is in italics. It shows the strength of the feeling that although this is the first time they have met properly, the mother/father (it could be interesting to discuss with the children whether they think this is the mother, father or another relative's voice) feels as if their relationship has already begun prior to the meeting.

[7] Why does the speaker want to be a better person? You could discuss this with the children. Do the people we love make us better people? How?

[8] The enjambment on this line is very significant. Up to this point, the poem has been very loving, but not very realistic – there have been lots of metaphors and hyperbolic language. Here, the single syllable 'but' changes the tone of the poem completely. It makes the reader slightly anxious...and the enjambment holds that anxiety slightly longer, as we shift down to the next line.

[9] The language of this line is plain. Simple. The phrase 'really hard to do' shows the difference between the feelings and emotions of the previous section of the poem and the actions of this line - there is a gap between emotion and action, caused by this line.

[10] What are the irritations that the speaker is talking about? You could discuss with the children the link between this line and line 11: to an oyster, the irritation becomes the pearl. Is there a significance there?

[11] Who is this 'us' that the speaker is talking about? Is it a generic 'us' as in everyone in the world? Or is it the 'us' of him/her and the baby? The personification of 'reality' as something that won't allow the speaker to be alone (either truly alone or alone with his/her baby) makes it seem nastier, somehow - it's an action on the part of the personified 'reality' to not allow this alone time.

[12] This is the only time this sort of repetition is used in this poem. This is also the only time this sort of punctuation is used in this poem. There seems to be a longing here - the speaker is longing to be alone with his/her baby. This is caused both by the repetition and also by the one word clause, separated by the colon (which is a stronger separation than a comma or semi-colon).

[13] What does this simile mean? You could discuss this with the children. 'Crystallised' could mean something both precious and beautiful. The idea of the 'pearl' could link back to the irritations the speaker mentioned previously. How could time crystallise? Is it because it seems as if time has stopped when they're together?

[14] This is a short clause with a huge amount of emotion in it. The image of being 'home' implies that the speaker feels that being with his/her baby/child is the safest and best place in the world.

[15] The speaker seems to be feeling anxious here to be sure that his/her child will understand that despite 'real life encroaching' and 'irritations in the word' and perhaps the breaking of the 'promises' (s)he made when the child was born (perhaps the speaker feels that (s)he has not always been the best parent - as every parent feels at one time or another) the speaker has always tried his/her best to keep the promise and to hold on to the feelings of love and joy created by the child's arrival in the world.

Stand Up For What You Know Is Right (a villanelle)

Stand up for what you know is right.
Don't be afraid of causing fuss.
Don't drift into a shameful night.

We all should face towards the light
The duty is for all of us.
Stand up for what you know is right.

In days to come, your children might
look up to you with artless trust.
Don't drift into a shameful night.

Work up your courage for the fight,
don't stand apart: be more robust.
Stand up for what you know is right.

When it feels hard to shine so bright
keep up your strength and readjust:
don't drift into a shameful night.

Allow your conscience to take flight
and guide you up out of the dust.
Stand up for what you know is right.
Don't drift into a shameful night.

Stand Up For What You Know Is Right - Annotated

A villanelle is a poem with a fixed form. It consists of five tercets (stanzas with three lines) followed by a quatrain (a stanza with four lines). The structure is very specific and very repetitive. There are always two repeating rhymes and two refrains (repeated lines or sections). The pattern of repetition that the refrains follow (shown in the 'refrain' column) is always the same – they first appear in lines 1 and 3 of the first stanza, then alternate at the end of each of the following stanzas until the final stanza, when they both appear again as a rhyming couplet on the final two lines.

Although it is not vital, most villanelles are written in iambic meter – this one is written in iambic tetrameter. This means that every line has eight syllables, broken down into four metrical feet consisting of two syllables each. A metrical foot in poetry is like a bar in music – it is how we separate rhythmic phrases of the same length. There are four metrical feet, called iambs, in each line of iambic tetrameter. Each iamb is a unit of rhythm which goes 'da-DUM'. Thus, a line of iambic tetrameter goes 'da-DUM da-DUM da-DUM da-DUM', where each 'da' and each 'DUM' is one syllable. A word such as 'away' has a natural iambic rhythm, because we put the emphasis on the 'way' when we pronounce it, we wouldn't say 'A-way', we would say 'a-WAY'.

The most famous example of a poem written in the villanelle form is Dylan Thomas' 'Do Not Go Gentle Into That Good Night'.

Line no.	Refrain	Rhyme scheme	Stand up for what you know is right.	Syllable Count
1	R1	A	Stand up[1] for what you know is right.[2]	8
2		B	Don't be afraid[3] of causing fuss.	8
3	R2	A	Don't drift into a shameful night.[4]	8
4		A	We all should face towards the light[5]	8
5		B	[5]The duty is for all of us.	8
6	R1	A	Stand up for what you know is right.	8
7		A	In days to come, your children might[6]	8
8		B	look up to you with artless trust.	8
9	R2	A	Don't drift into a shameful night.	8
10		A	Work up your courage for the fight,[7]	8
11		B	don't stand apart: be more robust.[8]	8
12	R1	A	Stand up for what you know is right.	8
13		A	When it feels hard to shine so bright[9]	8
14		B	keep up your strength and readjust:	8
15	R2	A	don't drift into a shameful night.	8
16		A	Allow your conscience to take flight[10]	8
17		B	and guide you up out of the dust.	8
18	R1	A	Stand up for what you know is right.	8
19	R2	A	Don't drift into a shameful night.	8

[1] The poem begins with an imperative – it makes it clear that this is a strong speaker who is taking charge straight away. Also, as this is the first refrain, this is repeated throughout the poem, in order to keep that strength and sense of authority going.

[2] The speaker is making an assumption here that the reader knows what 'is right'. It would be interesting to discuss this with the children – how do we know what is right? Is it something innate or something we learn? Do different people have different ideas of what is right and wrong?

[3] 'Don't be afraid' is another strong imperative statement – the speaker is inciting the reader to be brave and not worry about the consequences.

[4] The second refrain makes an interesting comparison to the first, because it is negative, as opposed to positive. Where the first refrain tells the reader what to do, the second tells the speaker what not to do. The alliteration on 'don't drift' is interesting also, because it highlights the word 'drift' – the implication of which is that it is easy to end up in a 'shameful night' without trying. The implication is that you have to try and make an effort to do the right thing because it's easy to just 'drift' into

([4] continued) doing the wrong thing or perhaps just being in the wrong by not having done the right thing. The morality of this would be interesting to discuss with the children - is it enough to just not do things wrong or do we have to actively do things right? The cliche of 'the road to Hell is paved with good intentions' could be something you use in this discussion. What does it mean? How does it apply to this poem?

[5] The personal pronoun here is inclusive – the speaker is including him/herself in this instruction. The modal verb 'should' is a strong one – again it speaks of a moral duty, as echoed by the word 'duty' on the following line and the repetition of the word 'all'.

[6] The modal verb here is interesting; we have changed from 'should' to 'might'. This is a slightly weaker statement, but in the context it is equally strong because you could argue that it is implying that the children 'might' have 'artless trust' in their parents, only if their parents do 'what you know is right'. This is an emotive idea which is quite affecting.

[7] This line has more images of 'doing the right thing' as being something we have to work towards. The words 'work', 'courage' and 'fight' attest to this.

[8] The colon here separates the line into two sections which are reflective of the two ideas in the two refrains – one negative and one positive.

[9] The metaphor 'shine so bright' is another strong one – the implication is that someone who is doing the right thing will be shining bright and visible and noticeable; perhaps this implies that the speaker doesn't think enough people do the right thing.

[10] The metaphor of someone's conscience as a bird could imply that it is something that will raise you up out of the ordinary. Perhaps another explanation is that a person's conscience is like an 'angel on your shoulder', as we say sometimes, so it is the good part of you striving for Heaven.

1. The smooth, sharp beak threatens coldly.
2. Intelligent, inquisitive eyes glare hungrily at the unsuspecting prey.
3. Powerful, patterned wings tense in anticipation: silence.
4. Tethered talons flex impatiently.
5. The prey is gone.

The Hawk - Annotated

This is an image poem. Image poems are really good ones to encourage the children to write, because you can be as supportive or as flexible as you feel the children need you to be and there is a simple start point for them to begin collating ideas. In brief, the children use a high quality image and write about it. However, they can use it in the sense of a very vague startpoint – 'tell me what this makes you think of' – or you can create a really specific set of criteria about the image – 'pick five features that you can see within the poem and use word association to come up with ten words which relate to each one...etc.' The poem can be super short or as long as the children (and/or you) want it to be. The idea of an image poem is to make children think really hard about their word choice. Does that adjective fully describe the real 'blueness' of the water? Does that verb fully portray the massive strength of the bird, if it should choose to move?

Line no.	The Hawk	Syllable Count
1	The smooth, sharp beak[1] threatens coldly.	8
2	Intelligent, inquisitive eyes[1] glare hungrily at the unsuspecting prey.	20
3	Powerful, patterned[1] wings tense in anticipation: silence[2].	15
4	Tethered talons[1] flex impatiently[3].	9
5	The prey is gone[4].	4

[1] Each line (except the last) begins with an alliterative description of one of the hawk's features – this is one way you could advise the children to structure their poems if they're unsure where to begin, because if they initially pick out a handful of features and then generate a handful of descriptive words or phrases for each features, they have a great place to start to construct their own poems. The alliteration can also emphasize a juxtaposition, so for example on line one where the speaker mentions the hawk's 'smooth, sharp beak', there is a comparison immediately between 'smooth' and 'sharp', which is made more obvious by the alliteration linking the two words together more closely.

[2] This one word holds the reader in anticipation very effectively. The colon separates the word from the rest of the sentence and the sibilance (repetition of 's' sounds) within the word 'silence' makes it sound like a person saying 'shh', which reflects the meaning of the word – these contribute to the feeling of holding your breath and waiting for something to happen.

[3] The word 'tethered' explains why the hawk is 'impatient' – he cannot get his prey because he is tied down. This is quite an interesting question raised in the poem – should he be tethered? Is this the speaker hinting that it is wrong to tie an animal up?

[4] The monosyllables (one-syllable words) on this line make it seem quite blunt. Perhaps the reader is supposed to feel sorry for the hawk. Using (and indeed repeating) the word 'prey' as opposed to saying 'rabbit' or 'mouse' makes us sympathise more with the hawk than the prey, as 'prey' is quite a vague and impersonal word.

The Ballad of Philemon and Baucis (pronounced phi-LEE-mon and BOR-siss)

Now hear the angels singing
of a wonderful love story.
Now gather round and smile
as you witness to their glory.

The quiet old Philemon
and his wife, Baucis the kind:
were both rewarded by the gods
for their generous, gentle minds.

A very long, long time ago,
in an age of Gods and heroes,
they lived a simple, rustic life:
she swept and cooked and he hoed

the garden, growing vegetables
to supply their worn old table.
In happiness, they lived their lives
as well as they were able.

One evening a loud knocking came
on the door of their poor house.
Two strangers sought some shelter
from Philemon and his spouse.

With generosity the two
old people let them in
and prepared to share their supper
without holding back a thing.

A veritable feast they now
created for their guests,
allowing them to have
whatever each guest liked the best.

One strange thing they noticed,
as they plied their guests with wine,
was that the pitcher never emptied,
regardless of the time.

With fearful glances Baucis
and Philemon realized
their honoured guests were gods!
Now this was really a surprise.

Worried that their supper
wouldn't please their lofty guests,
Philemon and his wife considered
what to do for best.

Outside the house they kept a goose
they now thought they should slaughter
to make a feast fit for a god.
They really thought they ought to.

Being old and slow, the couple
found it hard to catch the goose,
who, understandably, was most
determined to stay loose.

It fled into the house and there
it hid under the table.
With mournful honks it asked the gods
to do what they were able.

The gods (their names were Zeus and
Hermes) listened to its cries
and seeing the scared couple
couldn't help but sympathise.

"Don't worry," said the grateful gods,
"You have been more than gracious.
This humble feast was more welcome
than one more ostentatious."

Hermes and Zeus took Baucis
and Philemon up a hill,
in order to reward them
for their gesture of goodwill.

They looked back down upon the town.
Their eyes grew wide and scared.
The gods had swept the town away:
the valley now was bared.

With gentleness, the gods explained
"You two are rare as jewels:
the people of the valley were
all selfish, rude and cruel."

The flood the gods had sent
had shattered their old home,
so poor Philemon and his Baucis both
had nowhere left to go.

Compassionately, Zeus
and Hermes asked the couple if
the gods could give them anything
what now would be their wish?

With tenderly expressive eyes,
the couple merely smiled
and indicated, without words,
they did not fear exile.

Without a house, they had a home
in one another's hearts.
Through history, have there ever been
such comfortable sweethearts?

The gods were moved and heartened
by the gentle love they saw.
They pressed the couple kindly
to think of something to ask for.

Eventually, Philemon asked
to serve the gods as priest.
Baucis would be a priestess too
and, last but not least,

they asked to die together,
not one hour's length apart.
They couldn't bear to find that
they would separately depart

this life they'd shared so comfortably
and so the gods complied.
Then Baucis and Philemon
took up their new roles with pride.

For several years, they faithfully
served Zeus and Hermes well
and when at last the time had come
for them to say farewell

to earthly life, together they
departed, as they wished,
without a tear shed and
without one dear heartbeat missed.

Hermes and Zeus rewarded them
for their kind service by
transforming them to youthful trees
that reached up to the sky.

The trees entwined their branches,
and grew in each others' arms.
So Baucis and Philemon
never lost each others' charms.

The moral of this story's that
by being kind and good,
we make our own rewards in life
and death, just as we should.

A ballad is a poem which tells a story. It is often a love story, but not always. Ballads date back thousands of years and, in their earliest forms, were usually designed to be sung. For this reason, they have a fairly regular rhythm and a very regular rhyme scheme. The rhyme scheme is usually abXb, where X is a choice: it can rhyme with 'a' or it can not. Ballads are usually composed of four-line stanzas.

The story of Philemon and Baucis was originally told by Ovid in his 'Metamorphoses' (Book VIII). Ovid was a Roman poet. His Metamorphoses tell a variety of stories, all linked by the subject of love. Most of the stories were originally based on Greek myths.

The rhythm is fairly regular, to fit the song-like or chant-like ethos of the poem, so you can see that the number of syllables on each line are generally very similar. One thing you could do with the children is spot any particularly long or short lines and consider why they might be so short/ long. Is there a particularly important message that needed to be given in that line?

Line no.	Rhyme scheme	The Ballad of Philemon and Baucis (pronounced phi-LEE-mon and BOR-siss)	Syllable Count
1	A	Now[1] hear the angels singing	7
2	B	of a wonderful love story.	8
3	C	Now gather round and smile	7
4	B	as you witness to their glory.[2]	8
5	D	The quiet old[3] Philemon	7
6	E	and his wife, Baucis the kind:	7
7	F	were both rewarded by the gods	8
8	E	for their generous, gentle[4] minds.	7
9	G	A very long, long time ago,	8
10	H	in an age of Gods and heroes,[5]	8
11	I	they lived a simple, rustic life:	8
12	H	she swept and cooked and he hoed[6]	7
13	J	the garden,[6] growing vegetables	8
14	K	to supply their worn old table.	8
15	L	In happiness, they lived their lives[7]	8
16	K	as well as they were able.	7
17	M	One evening a loud knocking came	8
18	N	on the door of their poor house.	7
19	O	Two strangers sought some shelter [8]	7
20	N	from Philemon and his spouse.	7
21	P	With generosity the two	8
22	Q	old people let them in	6
23	R	and prepared to share their supper	8
24	Q	without holding back a thing.	7
25	S	A veritable feast they now	8
26	T	created for their guests,	6
27	U	allowing them to have	6
28	T	whatever each guest liked the best.[9]	8
29	V	One strange thing they noticed,	6
30	W	as they plied[10] their guests with wine,	7
31	X	was that the pitcher[11] never emptied,	9
32	W	regardless of the time.	6
33	Y	With fearful glances Baucis	7
34	Z	and Philemon realized	7
35	AA	their honoured guests were gods!	6
36	Z	Now this was really a surprise.[12]	8
37	BB	Worried that their supper	6
38	CC	wouldn't please their lofty guests,	7
39	DD	Philemon and his wife considered	9
40	CC	what to do for best.	5

[1] This time adverb makes this ancient story seem fresh and new – as if it's happening currently.

[2] This final line of the first stanza, combined with the first line's reference to 'angels singing' show that this is a traditional-style ballad. Ballads were traditionally supposed to tell quite noble stories of courage, love, sacrifice and strength and would often invoke the gods or angels to listen.

[3] These adjectives are strange ones to choose to describe the 'hero' of our story. There is a tone shift here, from the fully traditional in stanza 1 to this non-traditional hero in stanza 2. You could make a comparison between these adjectives and those on lines 11, 14, 45, 81 and 88. Throughout the poem, the couple are described in lots of nice ways, but never in a traditionally 'heroic' way.

[4] The alliteration here emphasizes the 'gentleness' and 'quietness' that the speaker is using to describe the two main characters. This reinforces the notion that they are a non-traditional hero and heroine.

[5] The use of this phrase sets Philemon and Baucis up as heroes – we know they were rewarded by the gods, we know they are 'old' and 'gentle', but now we have it confirmed to us that they are heroes.

[6] There is enjambment here, which could be used to imply that their life just carries on in the same way every day - not much changes for them. This doesn't seem negative though. The running on of the line into the next stanza could just be an indication that their lives have continued in the same way for a long time.

[7] The alliterative, repetitive quality of this phrase reiterates the implication started previously that Philemon and Baucis were simple people with a repetitive type of life.

[8] The sibilant quality of this line, with all its repeated 's' sounds, give an aural image of the night and, potentially, the conversation between the strangers and the couple. Perhaps it's because the conversation is held in whispers (hissing, like the 's' sounds would suggest). Perhaps they're whispering because it's night time. Perhaps it represents the wind in the trees, indicating that the night is windy and cold and unpleasant, hence the need for the strangers to seek shelter.

[9] The internal rhyme on this line of 'guest' and 'best' could imply that the couple are excellent hosts. Can the children come up with any other ideas as to the effect of this internal rhyme?

[10] This verb has connotations of plenty. The implication here is that the hosts were very generous.

The Ballad of Philemon and Baucis - Annotated

Line no.	Rhyme scheme	The Ballad of Philemon and Baucis (pronounced phi-LEE-mon and BOR-siss)	Syllable Count
41	EE	Outside the house they kept a goose	8
42	FF	they now thought they should slaughter	7
43	GG	to make a feast fit for a god.	8
44	FF	They really thought they ought to.[13]	7
45	HH	Being old and slow, the couple	8
46	II	found it hard to catch the goose,	7
47	JJ	who, understandably, was most [14]	8
48	II	[14] determined to stay loose.	6
49	KK	It fled into the house and there	8
50	LL	it hid under the table.	7
51	MM	With mournful honks it asked the gods[15]	8
52	LL	[15] to do what they were able.	7
53	NN	The gods (their names were Zeus and[16]	7
54	OO	Hermes)[16] listened to its cries	7
55	PP	and seeing the scared couple	7
56	OO	couldn't help but sympathise.	7
57	QQ	"Don't worry," said the grateful gods,[17]	8
58	RR	"You have been more than gracious.	7
59	SS	This humble[18] feast was more welcome	8
60	RR	than one more ostentatious."[18]	7
61	TT	Hermes and Zeus took Baucis	7
62	UU	and Philemon up a hill,	7
63	VV	in order to reward them	7
64	UU	for their gesture of goodwill.	7
65	WW	They[19] looked back down upon the town.	8
66	XX	Their[19] eyes grew wide and scared.	6
67	YY	The gods had swept the[19] town away:	8
68	XX	the[19] valley now was bared.	6
69	ZZ	With gentleness, the gods explained	8
70	AAA	"You two are rare as jewels:[20]	7
71	BBB	the people of the valley were	8
72	AAA	all selfish, rude and cruel."[21]	7
73	CCC	The flood the gods had sent	6
74	DDD	had shattered their old home,	6
75	EEE	so poor Philemon and his Baucis both	10
76	DDD	had nowhere left to go.	6
77	FFF	Compassionately,[22] Zeus	6
78	GGG	and Hermes asked the couple if	8
79	HHH	the gods could give them anything	8
80	GGG	what now would be their wish?	6
81	III	With tenderly expressive eyes,[23]	8
82	JJJ	[23] the couple merely smiled	6
83	KKK	[23] and indicated, without words,	8
84	JJJ	[23] they did not fear exile.	6
85	LLL	[23] Without a house, they had a home	8
86	MMM	[23] in one another's hearts.	6
87	NNN	[23] Through history, have there ever been	8
88	MMM	[23] such comfortable sweethearts?	6

[11] This is an old-fashioned noun for a wine jug, which fits into the ancient story effectively. It's the poet's/speaker's reminder to us that this story happened centuries ago.

[12] A surprise, perhaps, but not a huge shock. Back in ancient Greek/Roman times, the gods were much more likely to take it into their heads to visit mortals in this way. The stories seem to imply that it happened pretty regularly. So the noun 'surprise' here is quite accurate – surprising, but not completely out of character with what could be expected.

[13] The internal rhyme on this line, combined with the adverb 'really' and the fact that it is a repetition of what Philemon and Baucis are thinking, gives a sense of anxiety to this line. Philemon and Baucis are nervous (you can also see this from the word 'worried' on line 37) and they are talking themselves into doing something extravagant because they're scared of what the gods will do to them if the gods are displeased.

[14] There is a hint of comedy that creeps in here. The goose's feelings on the matter are 'understandable' and he is 'determined' to stay loose. This personification creates a comic effect, decreasing the tension that has been cause by Philemon and Baucis's anxiety over the gods' visit.

[15] The personification continues here. The goose is 'mournful' and has 'asked' the gods to help him stay alive. We can imagine the poor bird flapping around in panic and hiding under the table...the juxtaposition of the 'lofty' status of the gods and the lowly status of the silly goose creates more comedy, although we might be anxiously wondering what the gods will do – will they be offended?

[16] Discovering the names of the gods suddenly makes them more relatable. You could argue that this helps the reader feel a little relieved already, as the gods are no longer impersonal, scary beings, they have names and therefore less removed from Philemon and Baucis themselves.

[17] The alliteration here highlights the gratitude expressed by the gods. This is the ultimate reassurance for the reader and also shows how good Philemon and Baucis have been – they have been generous and kind enough to inspire gratitude in the gods!

[18] The juxtaposition of the adjectives 'humble' and 'ostentatious' seems to imply that there is more credit in a humble feast than in an 'ostentatious' or grand feast. The point that the gods (via the speaker, via the poet) seem to be making is that Philemon and Baucis hardly have anything and what they have they have given away freely and generously – there is more merit and credit in this than in giving what you can easily afford.

Line no.	Rhyme scheme	The Ballad of Philemon and Baucis (pronounced phi-LEE-mon and BOR-siss)	Syllable Count
89	OOO	The gods were moved and heartened	7
90	PPP	by the gentle love they saw.	7
91	QQQ	They pressed the couple kindly	7
92	PPP	to think of something to ask for.	8
93	RRR	Eventually, Philemon asked	8
94	SSS	to serve the gods as priest.	6
95	TTT	Baucis would be a priestess too	8
96	SSS	and, last but not the least,	6
97	UUU	they asked to die together,	7
98	VVV	not one hour's length apart.	7
99	WWW	They couldn't bear to find that	7
100	VVV	they would separately depart	7
101	XXX	this life they'd shared so comfortably	8
102	YYY	and so the gods complied.	6
103	ZZZ	Then Baucis and Philemon	7
104	YYY	took up their new roles with pride.	7
105	AAAA	For several years, they faithfully	8
106	BBBB	served Zeus and Hermes well	6
107	CCCC	and when at last the time had come	8
108	BBBB	for them to say farewell	6
109	DDDD	to earthly life, together they	8
110	EEEE	departed, as they wished,	6
111	FFFF	[24]without a tear shed and	7
112	EEEE	without one dear heartbeat missed.[24]	7
113	GGGG	Hermes and Zeus rewarded them	8
114	HHHH	for their kind service by	6
115	IIII	transforming them to youthful trees	8
116	HHHH	that reached up to the sky.	6
117	JJJJ	The trees entwined their branches,	7
118	KKKK	and grew in each others' arms.[25]	7
119	LLLL	So Baucis and Philemon	7
120	KKKK	never lost each others' charms.	7
121	MMMM	The moral of this story's that[26]	8
122	NNNN	by being kind and good,	6
123	OOOO	we make our own rewards in life	8
124	NNNN	and death, just as we should.	6

[19] There are lots of short sentences/phrases, which last exactly one line, in this stanza. Rhythmically, this changes the feeling of the poem – the tension is increased, as there are natural pauses created by the line and sentence breaks occurring together, so the effect is similar to having lots of short sentences in a paragraph of writing – it breaks it up and makes it feel jerky and tense. This reflects the events that have occurred in this

[20] The connotations of the noun used in this simile are of something precious and beautiful – the kindness and generosity of this couple is being likened to jewels. This shows the everyday heroism of this ostensibly 'ordinary' couple.

[21] This pattern of three emphasizes the difference between Philemon and Baucis and the other people in their valley.

[22] The poem continually attributes nice qualities to the gods. However, they have just destroyed a whole valley – you could discuss this with the children and see what their opinion of the gods really is. Perhaps they could think of some different adjectives and adverbs to describe the gods and their actions.

[23] These two stanzas are perhaps the most moving of the whole poem. The couple have just been made homeless – they have given away all their food to the gods and now they have nowhere to live, again, because of the gods. However, they are still completely content, because they have each other. The distinction made between 'house' and 'home' is a significant one, because their physical house has been destroyed, but they still feel like they have a safe place, because they have each other. The metaphor of having a home 'in one another's hearts' shows this. The rhetorical question at the end of the second stanza (lines 87-88) has an interesting adjective – 'comfortable' – implying that this is a relationship that is relaxed and comforting. It also could be said to have connotations of an actual house, so perhaps there is a double entendre here.

[24] The repetition here of 'without' and the grammatical constructions could be said to represent the dual nature of the relationship – it's representative of the fact that Philemon and Baucis were a two – they couldn't be separated.

[25] The personification here shows that the trees still retained the spirits of Baucis and Philemon.

[26] Do the children agree? What other morals could they take from this story?

Why, who makes much of a miracle?
As to me I know of nothing else but miracles,
Whether I walk the streets of Manhattan,
Or dart my sight over the roofs of houses toward the sky,
Or wade with naked feet along the beach just in the edge of the water,
Or stand under trees in the woods,
Or talk by day with any one I love, or sleep in the bed at night with any one I love,
Or sit at table at dinner with the rest,
Or look at strangers opposite me riding in the car,
Or watch honey-bees busy around the hive of a summer forenoon,
Or animals feeding in the fields,
Or birds, or the wonderfulness of insects in the air,
Or the wonderfulness of the sundown, or of stars shining so quiet and bright,
Or the exquisite delicate thin curve of the new moon in spring;
These with the rest, one and all, are to me miracles,
The whole referring, yet each distinct and in its place.

Miracles, by Walt Whitman - Annotated

Line no.	Miracles, by Walt Whitman[1]	Syllable Count
1	Why, who makes much of a miracle?[2]	9[3]
2	As to me I know of nothing else but miracles,	13
3	Whether I walk the streets of Manhattan,[4,5,6]	10
4	Or[7] dart my sight over[8] the roofs of houses toward the sky,	15
5	Or[7] wade with naked feet along[8] the beach just in the edge of the water,	18
6	Or[7] stand under[8] trees in the woods,	8[3]
7	Or[7] talk by day with any one I love, or sleep in the bed at night with any one I love,[9]	23
8	Or[7] sit at table at dinner with the rest,	11
9	Or[7] look at strangers opposite me riding in the car,	14
10	Or[7] watch honey-bees busy around the hive of a summer forenoon,	17
11	Or[7] animals feeding in the fields,[10]	9[3]
12	Or[7] birds, or the wonderfulness[11] of insects in the air,	14
13	Or[7] the wonderfulness[11] of the sundown, or of stars shining so quiet and bright,	18
14	Or[7] the exquisite delicate thin curve[12] of the new moon in spring;	16
15	These with the rest,[13] one and all, are to me miracles,	13
16	The whole referring,[14] yet each distinct and in its place.	13

[1] Walt Whitman (1819-1892) was a nineteenth century American poet, writer and journalist. He is often called the 'father of free verse', because he popularized poetry that was not only free verse but moved completely away from any sort of rhyme or consistent rhythm at all, in a very deliberate manner. He was a humanist, claiming to accept all gods and religions, but to subscribe to none. The theme of this poem – the miraculous in the everyday – was something he was very interested in. His poems were criticized for being too overtly sexual in nature, but were hugely influential, nonetheless.

[2] This rhetorical question at the beginning of the poem is the only sentence in the poem which isn't part of the incredibly long sentence that begins on line 2. The alliteration highlights the word 'miracle' and makes it clear that that is what we are discussing in this poem. It could also be a reference to religion and gently poking fun at the process of 'legitimising' miracles that happen in the name of a god or gods – to Whitman, everyday life is miraculous.

[3] There are only three lines with fewer than ten syllables in them in this poem. This makes them stand out a bit. You could discuss with the children why they think these have been made shorter. Perhaps it could be because what they are discussing is more simple than in some of the others - referring to nature, for example, or the rhetorical question at the beginning which is deliberately simple to contrast to the 'making much' that Whitman is gently making fun of.

[4] This line is the beginning of a very long sentence which comprises the entire rest of the poem. It goes some way to answering the rhetorical question on the first line, but makes it very clear that there is nothing in the world that Whitman doesn't regard as miraculous.

[5] Mentioning Manhattan specifically adds to the 'universal' nature of the experiences he is talking about, as Manhattan is a very metropolitan area, with rich and poor and everyone in between living side by side.

[6] Whitman considered himself an 'Everyman' – he was not a fan of social distinctions between people. The phrase 'walk the streets' is one which in a lot of ways universalizes his experience – he hasn't chosen to speak about a specialised experience, but one which everyone could have. This phrase also shows the 'everyday' nature of the miracles he is talking about.

[7] The repetition of the word 'or' at the beginning of these 11 lines shows how many different miracles Whitman sees in the world. This is a long list and it seems to be a deliberately long list to show how many phenomena in the world we can choose to find joy in.

[8] Juxtaposing these prepositions on succeeding lines shows the experiences Whitman is discussing going in every direction: up, across and down. In a very real sense, this shows how he is encompassing the whole world in his discussion of the miraculous.

[9] More juxtaposition on this line shows another contrast that Whitman is making between times: night and day. Both, to him, are miraculous. The repetition of the phrase 'with any one I love' highlights this. Additionally, this shows love to be miraculous.

[10] The alliteration of 'feeding' and 'fields' makes this line sound softer and gentler, in reflection of the image being created – a natural and beautiful one.

[11] The repetition of the word 'wonderfulness' is celebratory - this is the first time Whitman has allowed himself to use this kind of descriptive noun. This signals a change of tone. From a fairly basic list of actions and things, we now come to a section where Whitman is using language which gives the reader more of an insight into how he feels about these 'miracles'. You could ask the children to spot which words give us an idea of how he feels.

[12] Three adjectives! This could signal Whitman's narrator starting to get carried away. You could argue that he has started off trying to list these 'everyday miracles' in quite an ordinary way, perhaps to reflect the ordinary nature of them, but as he reaches the end of the poem he seems to get more excited and use more description. Perhaps the children could consider how this reflects a normal conversation - people do tend to get a bit more carried away as they warm to their subject.

[13] 'With the rest' is an interesting phrase – what does Whitman mean by it? Is it the rest of the world? What else could he mean? You could discuss this with the children.

[14] Whitman appears here to be talking about the entirety of life as a miracle. While each occurrence is miraculous in and of itself, alone, they all also each can be taken together to be 'the miracle of life'.

Love is like the wild rose-briar,
Friendship like the holly-tree –
The holly is dark when the rose-briar blooms
But which will bloom most constantly?
The wild rose-briar is sweet in spring,
Its summer blossoms scent the air;
Yet wait till winter comes again
And who will call the wild-briar fair?
Then scorn the silly rose-wreath now
And deck thee with the holly's sheen,
That when December blights thy brow
He may still leave thy garland green.

Love and Friendship, by Emily Brontë - Annotated

Line no.	Rhyme scheme	Love and Friendship, by Emily Brontë[1]	Syllable Count
1	A	Love is like the wild rose-briar,[2]	8
2	B	Friendship like the holly-tree[3] –	7
3	C	[4] The holly is dark when the rose-briar blooms	10
4	B	But which will bloom most constantly?[4]	8
5	D	The wild rose-briar is sweet in spring,[5]	8
6	E	Its summer [5] blossoms scent[6] the air;	8
7	F	Yet wait till winter [5] comes again	8
8	E	And who will call the wild-briar fair?	8
9	G	Then scorn the silly rose-wreath now[7]	8
10	H	[7] And deck thee with the holly's sheen,	8
11	G	That when December[5] blights thy brow[8]	8
12	H	He[9] may still leave thy garland green.[10]	8

[1] Emily Bronte (1818-1848) was one of four literary siblings (two other Bronte siblings died in childhood). Charlotte, Branwell, Emily and Anne (in age order) lived in a rural village in Yorkshire with their curate father, their mother having died when Emily was three. All were published poets and authors in their own lifetimes, but Charlotte and Emily are probably the best remembered, for their novels (Charlotte's Jane Eyre and Emily's Wuthering Heights). Wuthering Heights tells the story of Cathy and Heathcliff, two lovers whose unsuitable and damaging relationship ends in them destroying one another completely. Therefore, the message of this poem is quite interesting. Bronte compares love and friendship to two plants, asserting that the holly-tree (which she uses to represent friendship) is the more constant and reliable.

[2] This simile immediately sets up a slightly negative connotation to love. Not only is it 'wild', but it also is not just a rose, but a 'rose-briar'. A briar is a thorny bush, so the speaker is referring to not only the beauty of a rose, but the prickles of the bush.

[3] This simile could potentially be seen as not 100% positive, as holly is quite prickly. However, the difference is that the speaker hasn't focused on the negatives of the holly-tree, whereas (s)he did with the rose-briar. Also, mentioning the word 'tree' carries connotations of strength, as a tree is always going to be a more robust feature than a bush/ flower.

[4] These two lines make a direct comparison (which previously was only implied) between the tree and the briar. Initially, the comparison is favourable to the briar, but the speaker immediately goes against this with the conjunction 'but' on line 4. The rhetorical question, following this conjunction, suggests that the speaker is unimpressed with the 'bloom' of the rose and prefers the constancy of the holly-tree. The assonance in 'bloom', 'most' and 'constantly' reinforces this because it provides the constancy that the speaker is looking for.

[5] Using the seasons (and the month of December) extends the metaphor of the holly tree and the rose briar. The reference to how beautiful the rose is in spring and summer lasts only two lines and seems to suggest that the rose is wonderful – while it lasts. Spring and summer could be metaphors for the first flush of the relationship or perhaps for when times are good and happy. However, the longer section (six lines) referring to the fact that the rose will no longer be so beautiful in winter and the holly will seems to suggest that either once the first shine has worn off the relationship or perhaps when times are difficult and you are struggling, the rose will no longer be beautiful - or indeed there at all (as the blooms will die in cold weather). Instead, the people who will be there for you are your holly-tree friends, who are more 'constant'.

[6] There is a lovely sibilance here. You could discuss with the children what it could mean. Is it sibilant because it is creating an aural image of the summer and the buzzing of the bees and the whispering of the wind? Could it be an aural image of the whispering that goes on between lovers – as in the cliché 'whispering sweet nothings'? It might even be a hiss of disapproval, because the speaker is disapproving of the rose's blossoms as being over the top and showy.

[7] These two lines are imperative. The speaker has chosen to instruct the reader to 'scorn' the rose and 'deck' him/herself with the holly instead. Interestingly, the speaker has chosen to refer to a rose 'wreath', which is a potentially funereal image. The adjective 'silly' is quite judgemental - the speaker is making it quite clear what her opinion is of love versus friendship!

[8] There is more alliteration here, which is quite plosive and violent. One wonders what the speaker may have experienced to make him/her feel that December brings a blight. However, there is also deliberate ambiguity here, as a 'blight' is a specific term for a symptom of various diseases that affect plants and effectively kill them very quickly.

[9] The personification of December is interesting, because one wonders whether the speaker is perhaps linking December with the rose – perhaps where the rose represents love, December represents the lover or the lover's abandonment. This would therefore imply that December (the lover) 'blights' his/ her 'brow' by leaving him/her, but his/her 'garland' will still be 'green' because (s)he will still have his/her friends.

[10] The alliteration on the final two words makes the metaphor really stand out – what is someone's 'garland'? You could discuss this with the children. Perhaps it could be your surroundings. It could possibly be your heart or your life in general.

Storm in the Black Forest, by D. H. Lawrence

Now it is almost night, from the bronzy soft sky
jugfull after jugfull of pure white liquid fire, bright white
tipples over and spills down,
and is gone
and gold-bronze flutters beat through the thick upper air.

And as electric liquid pours out, sometimes
a still brighter white snake wriggles among it, spilled
and tumbling wriggling down the sky:
and then the heavens cackle with uncouth sounds.

And the rain won't come, the rain refuses to come!

This is the electricity that man is supposed to have mastered
chained, subjugated to his own use!
supposed to!

Storm in the Black Forest, by D. H. Lawrence - Annotated

Line no.	Storm in the Black Forest,[1] by D. H. Lawrence[2]	Syllable Count[3]
1	Now it is almost night, from the bronzy soft sky[4]	12
2	jugfull after jugfull of pure white liquid fire, bright white[5]	14
3	tipples over and spills down,	7
4	and is gone	3
5	and gold-bronze flutters beat through the thick upper air.	12
6	And as electric liquid pours out,[6] sometimes	11
7	a still brighter white snake wriggles[7] among it, spilled	12
8	and tumbling wriggling down the sky:	8
9	and then the heavens cackle with uncouth sounds.[8]	11
10	And the rain won't come, the rain refuses to come![9,10]	12
11	This is the electricity that man is supposed to have mastered	17
12	chained, subjugated to his own use![10]	9
13	supposed to![10,11]	3

[1] The title of the poem describes an event which Lawrence witnessed: he travelled around Europe for several years and was in the Black Forest (in Germany) in 1929 when a huge storm hit.

[2] D. H. Lawrence (1885-1930) was an English novelist, primarily, but he also wrote plays, poetry and essays as well as being a painter. He had some very controversial opinions and was widely considered to be a rather scandalous writer and person. One thing he was particularly voluble about was modernity and the effect of modern inventions on people's lives. This is something that comes across in this poem. He saw industrialization as a dehumanizing process and was very against all the new machinery that he saw emerging in the early twentieth century. This theme runs throughout this poem.

[3] The length of the lines is very inconsistent. You could argue that this reflects the storm – it is unpredictable and wild, just like the structure of this poem.

[4] These two adjectives used to describe the sky seem deliberately misleading, when compared to the rest of the poem. It seems as if the sky is gentle and dark and getting ready for the 'night' which is mentioned in the beginning fo the line. However, after this, the sky is rent apart by lightning. Perhaps this is showing the reader how quickly the storm came on; initially everything seemed calm and quiet, but out of nowhere the lightning came and awed him/her with its destructive, yet beautiful power.

[5] The repetition on this line is quite striking – both 'jugfull' and 'white' are repeated, and there is internal rhyme ('bright' and 'white'). This could be said to represent the length of the storm – it is going on and on, seemingly without end. This is also a very visual metaphor; Lawrence describes the lightning as almost a waterfall of white fire. There is so much of it, it would seem, that it loses its individuality in regards to specific sheets of lightning and becomes simply one great monster storm!

[6] This metaphor is very similar to the one on line 2; it continues the image of the lightning as liquid; continuous.

[7] This metaphor gives life to the lightning; the forked lightning strikes are 'snakes' – an image which, it could be argued, has connotations of evil. However, there is a literal visual connection here too, between the forked lightning and the forked tongue of the snake.

[8] The personification here is interesting – we wouldn't usually imagine the heavens (which tend to carry connotations of angels and god and peace) cackling – this is a verb we might associate with evil witches, like in Macbeth. This juxtaposition, coupled with the adjective 'uncouth', which reinforces the negative connotations of 'cackle', creates a sense of madness – perhaps Lawrence is implying that heaven has gone mad, gone wild or lost its mind. You could also link this to the image of the 'snake' on line 7.

[9] The repetition here implies that the speaker is perhaps longing for the rain to come, to break the tension of the storm. However, the repetition is not perfect; one word is different the second time around. The verb 'refuses' is very powerful here. It shows that nature is not subject to man. Again, this is the speaker showing how powerless (s)he is in the face of the power of nature.

[10] The use of exclamation marks shows us the speaker's emotions – (s)he is excited and, perhaps, feeling rather over-awed by the majesty of the storm. This interpretation fits with the tone of the poem overall, as the speaker is clearly linking the work of nature to the work of man and saying how much greater nature's power is than that of man.

[11] The repetition of 'supposed to' is heavily sarcastic; the speaker is making it very clear that (s)he doesn't believe that man has 'mastered' or 'subjugated' electricity. Indeed, the whole poem shows that the speaker believes that nature has much more power than man.

Eldorado, by Edgar Allan Poe

Gaily bedight,
A gallant knight,
In sunshine and in shadow,
Had journeyed long,
Singing a song,
In search of Eldorado.

But he grew old-
This knight so bold-
And o'er his heart a shadow
Fell as he found
No spot of ground
That looked like Eldorado.

And, as his strength
Failed him at length,
He met a pilgrim shadow-
"Shadow," said he,
"Where can it be-
This land of Eldorado?"

"Over the Mountains
Of the Moon,
Down the Valley of the Shadow,
Ride, boldly ride,"
The shade replied-
"If you seek for Eldorado!"

Eldorado, by Edgar Allan Poe - Annotated

Line no.	Rhyme scheme[1]	Eldorado,[2] by Edgar Allan Poe[3]	Syllable Count[4]
1	A	Gaily bedight,[5]	4
2	A	A gallant knight,	4
3	B	In sunshine and in shadow,[6,7]	7
4	C	Had journeyed long,	4
5	C	Singing a song,	4
6	B	In search of Eldorado.[8]	7
7	D	But he grew old-	4
8	D	This knight so bold-	4
9	B	And o'er his heart a shadow[6]	7
10	E	Fell as he found	4
11	E	No spot of ground	4
12	B	That looked like Eldorado.	7
13	F	And, as his strength	4
14	F	Failed him at length,	4
15	B	He met a pilgrim shadow[6,9] -	7
16	G	"Shadow," said he,	4
17	G	"Where can it be-	4
18	B	This land of Eldorado?"	7
19	H	"Over the Mountains	5
20	H	Of the Moon,	3
21	B	Down the Valley of the Shadow,[6]	8
22	I	Ride, boldly ride,"	4
23	I	The shade replied-	4
24	B	"If you seek for Eldorado!"	8

[1] The poem is made up of four sestets (six-line stanzas). Each has a very regular rhyme and regularly repeats the words 'shadow' in the middle and 'Eldorado' at the end. You could discuss with the children why they think the poem is so regular. Is it reflective of the knight's continuous hunt for Eldorado? Is it to reflect the sorts of poems that were written in mediaeval times? Is it to suggest the sound of the horse's rhythmic hoofbeats, as the knight goes about his search?

[2] El Dorado is the mythical 'City of Gold' searched for over the centuries by various explorers. It is probably based on misinterpretations and exaggerated stories told by European colonizers of South America. When Spanish explorers reached South America in the early 16th century, they were told stories of a native tribe living in the Andes mountains. The held initiation ceremonies at Lake Guatavita whenever they had a new chief. This involved the new ruler being covered in gold dust. The tribe would then throw gold and jewels into the lake to appease the god that they believed lived under the water. The Spanish explorers began calling the chief 'El Dorado' (The Golden/Gilded One). In the late 15th century, the ceremonies stopped when the tribe was conquered by another tribe. The Spanish explorers found Lake Guatavita in 1545, they tried to drain it, finding hundreds of pieces of gold along the edge of the lake. However, they weren't able to access the bulk of the treasure (or what they presumed was the location of the bulk of the treasure) in the middle of the lake. This treasure turned to legend, and gradually, over the years, evolved (as these stories are wont to do) into a 'city' of gold.

[3] Edgar Allan Poe (1809-1849) was an American poet, author and literary critic. His work forms a large part of the American literary canon and is largely Gothic in style. He often wrote about death and the afterlife, in many different ways, and this poem is no exception. The knight, at the end of the poem, is advised by the 'pilgrim shadow' to ride to the 'Valley of the Shadow', which is usually taken to be the 'Valley of the Shadow of Death' mentioned in Psalm 23 in the Bible. It has been said that this poem was written as Poe's reposnse to the 'Gold Rush' which was happening in California at the time he wrote the poem. He is clearly advising readers against the obsession with wealth and gold which characterised the Gold Rush. The poem was also one of his last, so it may be that he used it as a vehicle to give his readers advice, based on the wisdom he accrued over his years. He was, perhaps, looking forward to the 'Eldorado' of wisdom and understanding that he would find after his death.

[4] The rhythm is very regular, just like the rhyme scheme. There is a slight change in the final stanza – why do the children think this is? Does this reflect the end of the knight's life and his transition into death? Or the realization that he has at the end of his life of the fruitless nature of his search?

[5] Bedight is an old-fashioned word that means 'adorned' or 'decorated'.

[6] The word 'shadow' is repeated on the third line of each stanza. However, each time it carries a different meaning. First, it is a literal shadow, set in opposition to the 'sunshine'. Second, it is a metaphorical shadow to show the knight's depression and despondency at not finding Eldorado. Third, it refers to a ghost (shadow was a euphemism for ghost in the nineteenth century) who meets the knight and advises him on how to find Eldorado. Fourth and lastly, it refers to the 'Valley of the Shadow', which, as mentioned, is usually accepted as 'the Valley of the Shadow of Death' mentioned in Psalm 23, and therefore is a reference to death.

[7] In addition to the literal interpretation of this line (that the knight rode on whatever the weather/time of day), there is also a metaphorical reading of this line. Perhaps this is a metaphor for the positive and negative experiences of the knight's life - or indeed of anyone's life. This then links to the contrast between 'shadow' and 'Eldorado'. Perhaps the overall contrast is between the sadness of death and the advantages that the speaker (and the knight, after his conversation with the shadow) perceive after death.

[8] Eldorado appears at the end of the last line of each stanza. Perhaps this is Poe's hint that Eldorado is an ultimate destination, not a place you can find along the way, i.e. Eldorado is heaven. Or perhaps it's Poe's hint that Eldorado is a state of mind we attain after a journey, i.e. Eldorado is a metaphorical place of spiritual treasures that we accumulate throughout our lives; the wisdom and peace we (hopefully) attain at the end of our lives is the treasure we find in Eldorado.

[9] As mentioned previously, this use of the word 'shadow' seems to refer to a ghost, as 'shadow' was a euphemism for ghost in the nineteenth century. However, the word 'pilgrim' is interesting here. A pilgrim is on a religious quest/journey. Is this shadow on a religious quest? Perhaps it is a ghost who is searching for Eldorado - one which is stuck in limbo. Perhaps this whole section is a metaphor for the knight talking to himself; reflecting on his life and realising the only way to have the spiritual treasure he craves is in death. Thus, the 'pilgrim shadow' is the knight's soul/inner self.

What's the best thing in the world?
June-rose, by May-dew impearled;
Sweet south-wind, that means no rain;
Truth, not cruel to a friend;
Pleasure, not in haste to end;
Beauty, not self-decked and curled
Till its pride is over-plain;
Light, that never makes you wink;
Memory, that gives no pain;
Love, when, so, you're loved again.
What's the best thing in the world?
- Something out of it, I think.

Line no.	Rhyme scheme[1]	The Best Thing in the World,[2] by Elizabeth Barrett Browning[3]	Syllable Count
1	A	What's the best thing in the world?[4]	7
2	A	June-rose, by May-dew[5] impearled;	7
3	B	Sweet south-wind, that means no rain;	7
4	C	Truth,[6] not cruel[7] to a friend;	7
5	C	Pleasure[6], not in haste to end;	7
6	A	Beauty[6], not self-decked and curled	7
7	B	Till its pride is over-plain;[8]	7
8	D	Light[6], that never makes you wink;[9]	7
9	B	Memory[6], that gives no pain;	7
10	B	Love[6], when, so, you're loved again.[10]	7
11	A	What's the best thing in the world?[4]	7
12	D	-[11] Something out of it, I think.[12]	7

[1] This poem has a very odd rhyme scheme. Perhaps this is reflective of individuality; you could argue that it is a collection of different ideas, linked together in strange ways, each of which combine to create one thing (the poem). This reinforces the idea that Barrett Browning might be referring to a spiritual quality within all the beautiful and wonderful things in life, which is 'the best thing in the world' (yet somehow otherworldly, as evidenced by the final line of the poem).

[2] This poem is characteristic of Barrett Browning's work in its spirituality. It is essentially a list poem in which she recounts a number of things which seem to compete for the title of 'the best thing in the world'. However, she ends by stating that 'the best thing in the world' is 'something out of it, I think'. Perhaps she is saying that none of the things she listed is the best. Perhaps she is saying that they are all wonderful, but it's some ineffable spiritual quality in all of them which makes them so wonderful and it's that spiritual (otherworldly) quality that is 'the best thing in the world'. You could discuss this with the children.

[3] Elizabeth Barrett Browning (1806-1861) was an English poet. She was one of the most famous poets both in Britain and America in her lifetime. She married the poet Robert Browning in 1846 and moved, with him, to Italy, in an attempt to lessen the severity of the chronic illness she suffered with from the age of 15. There, she had a son, Robert (known as Pen), and there she died of her illness when her son was 12. Her poetry is extremely spiritual and much of it is quite political, calling for (amongst other things) the abolition of slavery and child labour.

[4] The use of this rhetorical question both at the beginning and at the end seems to, somehow, book-end the poem. It keeps the reader thinking about the answer (and, therefore, the real meaning of the whole poem – exploring the wonder of the world).

[5] Logically, if the 'June-rose' is impearled by 'May-dew', this must be the first day of June, with the dew from the previous night (the last night of May) still on it. This is a very specific time of the year to mention – perhaps it's the turn of the seasons from a spring month to a summer month (as spring turns to summer in June) that the speaker is saying is so wonderful.

[6] Several of the 'best things' that the speaker mentions are abstract concepts which (s)he qualifies – not just truth, but truth that isn't cruel, not just memory, but memory that brings no pain – these simple concepts, with the negatives removed, are perfect - the 'best' things in the world.

[7] In order to keep the rhythm consistent, it is necessary to pronounce this word with two syllables: 'cru-el'.

[8] By over-plain, we can infer that the speaker means 'obvious' here. She is taking about beauty that is overdone- overly made up or decked out in lots of frilly clothes, to show that the person is overly proud of their appearance. To the speaker, this obvious pride spoils things. Beauty must be pure to be 'the best thing in the world'.

[9] 'Wink', in the nineteenth century, was often used to be synonymous with the word 'blink' – the idea, therefore, of this line is that light is only 'the best' if it doesn't make you blink and hurt your eyes.

[10] 'Again', in this context, means 'as well'. The speaker is talking about reciprocal love – where each person loves the other – as opposed to unrequited love – where one person loves, but is not loved in return – which would be painful and, clearly, not the 'best thing in the world'.

[11] The dash here is unnecessary – this line is not only a separate entity by virtue of being a line on its own, but also it's a sentence on its own, following the question mark on the previous line. The inclusion of the dash therefore gives an even greater degree of separation. Perhaps this is because the speaker is moving from talking about things 'in the world' to something 'out of it'. (S)he needs to ensure a full separation not just by line or sentence, but also by the dash.

[12] This is the first reference we have in the poem to an 'I'. This personal pronoun gives the first hint that the speaker is giving their own opinion. The previous ideas have been just that - ideas. They are not necessarily reflective of the speaker's own opinion. (Although they may still be - it is up to the children to decide what they think about that!)

YEAR 6

Alphabet England

As every educated girl and every knowledgeable
Boy who lives in any of the UK's four
Countries naturally knows,
Danes and Angles once roamed round
Every corner of this green and pleasant land.
From these two very different races,
Gradually, a peaceful deal (don't ask me
How!) was struck and
In a great stone castle
(Just near Gloucester)
King Athelstan was crowned.
Lots of kings were
Married then to lots of queens,
Not only from this country
Or its neighbours, but from
Pretty far-flung corners
(Quite remote ones) of the world.
Relationships got ever closer,
Slowly through the decades,
Turning all the diverse tribes into a
United Kingdom, which eventually started looking
Very similar to ours today. A few big
Wars and floods and famines separate us from our
Xylogenous ancestors, but the
Years have shown us this: as we
Zigzag through the centuries, together is better.

Alphabet England - Annotated

An alphabet poem's first line begins with A, and each subsequent line begins with the following letter of the alphabet, right through to Z. There is no particular scheme as to rhyme or rhythm.

There is no particular rhythm to this poem. The lines are of seemingly random lengths. Is this, perhaps, to represent the history of the UK? Perhaps you could say it's to represent the different centuries passing – some full with lots of events, some seeming to whizz past without much changing. Perhaps it could be to represent the different people of the UK; all different, but making up a societal whole which works well together.

Line no.	Alphabet England	Syllable Count
1	As every educated girl and every knowledgeable[1]	15
2	Boy who lives in any of the UK's four	11
3	Countries naturally knows,	7
4	Danes and Angles once roamed round[2]	7
5	Every corner of this green and pleasant land.[3]	11
6	From these two very different races,	9
7	Gradually, a peaceful deal (don't ask me	10
8	How!)[4] was struck and	4
9	In a great stone castle	6
10	(Just near Gloucester)	4
11	King Athelstan[5] was crowned.	6
12	Lots of kings were[5]	4
13	Married then to lots of queens,[6]	7
14	Not only from this country	7
15	Or its neighbours, but from	6
16	Pretty far-flung corners	6
17	(Quite remote ones) of the world. [7]	7
18	Relationships got ever closer,	9
19	Slowly through the decades,	6
20	Turning all the diverse tribes[8] into a	10
21	United Kingdom, which eventually started looking	14
22	Very similar to ours today. A few big	12
23	Wars and floods and famines[9] separate us from our	12
24	Xylogenous[10] ancestors, but the	9
25	Years have shown us this:[11] as we[12]	7
26	Zigzag[13] through the centuries, together is better.[14]	13

[1] Slightly sarcastic tone, especially when added to the word 'naturally' in line 3; is the poet implying that this is actually not common knowledge? Why? Should we be expected to know?

[2] Alliteration. Interesting choice of verb. Why 'roamed'? Perhaps because the tribes were explorers and conquerors?

[3] A quotation from the poem 'And did those feet in ancient times', by William Blake (you may know it better as the hymn 'Jerusalem' – the poem was put to music and re-titled by Sir Hubert Parry in 1916). This refers to the beauty of England.

[4] Slightly comic tone caused by this aside (brackets show it is an aside); made personal by the use of the personal pronoun 'me'. What does this imply about the relations between the Danes and Angles? Perhaps it was very violent, as the poet suggests that (s)he doesn't know how peace could have been reached?

[5] First King of the English, from 927-939 (approx.). He united England for the first time.

[6] Slightly dismissive/casual tone? A summary of the history of several centuries: gives it a rather 'soap opera' feel – it was all about the relationships. Perhaps discuss how fitting a description this is?

[7] Why does this matter? What's the significance of the kings/queens marrying people from all over the world? Perhaps if we link this to the final line and the poem's 'moral', we can suggest that this implies that England has always been accepting of marriage between people of different cultures? (To what extent this is true is a matter for dicsussion)

[8] Use of the noun 'tribe' implies a certain lack of civilization, potentially. The word carries connotations of barbarism. (Or does it, nowadays? It's an interesting discussion)

[9] Pattern of three: 'wars, floods, famines'. Again, quite a casual tone for big, life-changing events. Is this to show the huge amount of time we are dealing with and how even hugely significant events become subsumed with the weight of history?

[10] Meaning: living in or on wood. (A reference to wooden houses built hundreds of years ago.)

[11] The colon implies that something important is coming. Is this the moral/message of the poem?

[12] Personal pronoun; makes the reader feel they're part of the history of the UK, along with the poet him/herself.

[13] An interesting choice of verb. Why are we 'zigzagging;? What is the significance of this choice of verb?

[14] Is this the poem's 'moral'? What does this mean for 21st Century society? It could be seen as a succinct, three word summary of multiculturalism

Happiness

I'll fight for you, with all my power and will.
I shall not let the world rip you away.
When darkness falls, you shall be with me still.
I cannot let you leave: you have to stay
with me and be my love and be my prize.
I could not live without you here to hold.
I read the doubt that bruises both your eyes,
but we will be together till we're old.
Your heart is a wild bird, tethered to me
and I'll enclose you safely, keep you here.
Give up this vain attempt to set it free.
The only thing to overcome is fear.
When you accept that you were made for me,
you will begin to realise you're happy.

Happiness - Annotated

Originally, sonnets came from Italy and gradually evolved to mean a fourteen line poem with a regular rhyme scheme and rhythm. When sonnets first came to England, they were written in the Italian style; a style known as Petrarchan. Later, English poets, including Shakespeare, adopted and adapted the sonnet form into the most usual form known today, which is (perhaps unfairly, as Shakespeare did not invent it) known as the Shakespearean sonnet. Sonnets have a very specific rhythm and rhyme scheme. They are usually about love.

A Shakespearean sonnet has an ABAB rhyme scheme throughout, until the final two lines, which are a rhyming couplet.

A Shakespearean sonnet is written in iambic pentameter. This means that every line has ten syllables, broken down into five metrical feet consisting of two syllables each. A metrical foot in poetry is like a bar in music – it is how we separate rhythmic phrases of the same length. There are five metrical feet, called iambs, in each line of iambic pentameter. Each iamb is a unit of rhythm which goes 'da-DUM'. Thus, a line of iambic pentameter goes 'da-DUM da-DUM da-DUM da-DUM da-DUM', where each 'da' and 'DUM' is one syllable. A word such as 'away' has a natural iambic rhythm, because we put the emphasis on the 'way' when we pronounce it, we wouldn't say 'A-way', we would say 'a-WAY'. If you emphasise the natural rhythm of speech when you read a sonnet, you will notice the iambic rhythm immediately.

Line no.	Rhyme scheme	Happiness	Syllable Count
1	A	I'll fight for you,[2] with all my power and will.[3]	10
2	B	I shall[4] not let the world rip [1] you away.[5]	10
3	A	When darkness[1] falls, you shall[4] be with me still.	10
4	B	I cannot[4] let you leave: you have to stay	10
5	C	with me and be my love and be my prize.	10
6	D	I could[4] not live without you here to hold.[1]	10
7	C	I read the doubt that bruises[1] both your eyes,[6]	10
8	D	but we will[4] be together till we're old.[7]	10
9	E	Your heart is a wild bird,[8] tethered[1] to me	10
10	F	and I'll[4] enclose[1] you safely, keep you here.	10
11	E	Give up[1] this vain attempt to set it free.	10
12	F	The only thing to overcome is fear.[1]	10
13	G	When you accept that you were made for me,	10
14	G	you will[4] begin to realise you're happy.[9]	10

[6] This metaphor is quite scary – it refers to violence in 'bruises' and could be a double entendre implying that the speaker has been quite violent towards his/her partner.

[7] There is a subtle play on words here, wherein the reader could ask him/herself what the speaker means by 'old'. Is this literally old in terms of age? Or is it feeling old and weary and beaten down, as the speaker's partner possibly might feel in a destructive relationship like the one in the poem.

[8] This metaphor shows the speaker's partner seems to want to get away. You could link this to the images of being 'tethered' later on this line or 'enclosed' on line 10. The speaker seems to want to trap his/her partner into the relationship like a wild animal being caged.

[9] This final rhyming couplet is almost the most sinister section of the poem. The speaker is implying that once his/her partner just 'gives up' (as he or she is asked to do on line 11) (s)he will 'accept' the situation and start to live with it. It seems as if the speaker is completely deluded in imagining that his/her partner will be 'happy'.

[1] There are some really negative images scattered throughout this poem. There is violence in 'rip', 'bruises' and 'fear', combined with the idea of being imprisoned in 'hold', 'tethered' and 'enclose'. There are also pleas for the person the speaker is addressing to 'give up' and give in to the 'darkness' (s)he will bring. You could discuss this with the children - perhaps just give them these words and ask them to consider what this relationship is like. Or ask them to find negative words from the poem. The negative images imply that this is quite a destructive relationship. The speaker's partner seems to want to break away and the speaker is refusing to allow him/her to. It's quite a dark and dangerous relationship. You could discuss this with the children and talk about what makes a healthy relationship (perhaps link to SMSC/PSHE curriculum).

[2] The poem immediately begins with quite an aggressive metaphor. You could argue that this is unusual for a love poem. However, the speaker is clearly addressing someone specific: the personal pronouns tell us that. Therefore, perhaps the speaker is talking about fighting for the relationship, which is an accepted metaphor and could be said to demonstrate his/her strength of feeling.

[3] The speaker seems to be setting him/herself up as a strong, dominant person here. The verb 'fight' combined with the nouns 'power' and 'will' create a sense of strength and dominance.

[4] There are lots of modal verbs in this poem. The speaker uses them about him/herself usually. It is only on the last line that it is turned around on the person (s)he is speaking to. The use of these particular modal verbs shows the force with which the speaker is talking. Each one is very definite and forceful. This leads to an overall tone of dominance and power, with the speaker appearing extremely authoritative, but potentially in a fairly negative way. You could discuss this with the children - based on the modal verbs, do they think the speaker is nice or not nice?

[5] This metaphor is interesting, because it implies that there are forces trying to keep the 'lovers' apart. Perhaps 'the world' is a metaphor for their families and/or friends? Perhaps it's circumstances, such as the speaker's partner being offered a job in a new location or wanting to go travelling or something which means their relationship might be put under strain.

In the Blink of an Eye

1. A delicate ball of green and blue hangs motionless in the art gallery of my mind. The blackness of space is freckled with pinprick stars and I half expect the world to blink like a gritted eye. What would be expelled from that vast blinking sphere? Belching factories and skittering lorries? Heaven-bound jets and flickering power stations? What irritates you, Mother, the most? Or perhaps it's none of these. Perhaps our miraculous, forgiving, maternal host can tolerate the abuses we parasites enact on her flesh, but, like any mother, she weeps to see the abuses her children enact on one another. Can her tears wash away the violence, the intolerance, the fear? Or will she close her eye to it like we do?

In the Blink of an Eye - Annotated

A prose poem is a really interesting one to do, because you can spark a discussion with the children as to what a poem actually is. Often, children get so focused on layout that they forget that what makes a poem is your use of language. A prose poem uses the language of poetry, but the layout of prose. It looks like a paragraph of a novel, but has a focus on imagery and lyricism, meter, rhythm, description and sometimes even rhyme.

Line no.

In the Blink of an Eye[1]

A fragile[2] ball of green and blue hangs motionless[3] in the art gallery of my mind.[4] The blackness of space is freckled[5] with pinprick stars and I half expect the world to blink like a gritted eye.[6] What would be expelled from that vast blinking sphere? Belching factories and skittering lorries? Heaven-bound jets and flickering power stations?[7] What irritates[8] you, Mother, the most?[9] Or perhaps[10] it's none of these. Perhaps[10] our miraculous, forgiving, maternal[11] host can tolerate the abuses[13] we parasites[12] enact on her flesh, but, like any mother, she weeps to see the abuses[13] her children enact on one another.[14] Can her tears wash away the violence, the intolerance, the fear? Or will she close her eye to it like we do?[15]

[1] What can happen 'in the blink of an eye'? This is a discussion you could have with the children. Literally, what could happen and metaphorically what could happen? Why is this a cliché? What does the speaker imply could happen in the blink of an eye? Is it the destruction of a planet? You could discuss the concept of time and how differently time seems to pass on different occasions, e.g. when you're bored or when you're rushing because you're late. Based on this idea, what could happen in the blink of an eye, based on the perspective of the earth? It's billions of years old – so is the blink of an eye 100 years? Or is it a millennium? Or more?

[2] Why is this adjective used at the beginning of this poem? What makes the world 'fragile'? It's not the first thing we think of when it comes to a huge planet, so why has the speaker chosen to use this description? You could discuss this with the children. Perhaps the speaker is indicating that the world is more fragile than we think and we need to take care of it. Perhaps it is the image of the world that is fragile – why could this be?

[3] Why 'hangs motionless'? The world is constantly moving. Is this a hint that there is something wrong with the world? Perhaps it's an indication that the speaker wants the world to pause a moment to consider the way the future is going. Perhaps it's an indication that the speaker wants the world to stop the bad things that are happening in it (which (s)he goes on to discuss later)

[4] What a lovely image! What does the speaker mean by it? Perhaps it's the idea of memories being visual; so a memory conjures up a picture in your mind. Perhaps it could be a surreal art gallery, full of odd objects and weird sculptures? perhaps it's the imagination, rather than memory – the speaker is imagining the world, rather than actually seeing it.

[5] Personification – space seems like a person here, with a freckled face.

[6] This reinforces the personification begun with the word 'freckled'. It's a horrible-sounding simile, because we know having grit in your eye is an awful feeling. It might also make us wonder what the 'grit' is. Could it be us (humans)? Is it the pollution we cause? You could discuss this with the children.

[7] There are two possible interpretations of the word 'irritate': either a physical irritation, like a rash, or something in your eye, or a mental/emotional irritation. This is, therefore, a double entendre, as both meanings are appropriate and implied.

[8] Rhetorical questions. These continue the discussion started in the previous sentence about what the 'grit' is. These sentences give options about what might be got rid of by the blink of the world.

[9] There is a big change here. Suddenly the speaker is asking a direct question to 'Mother'. Who is this 'Mother'? You could discuss this with the children. It seems fairly clear that the speaker is addressing the world. So is this Mother Earth? Or Mother Nature? Or are they the same thing?

[10] Repetition here – the speaker is speculating as to what the earth is 'irritated' by.

[11] Pattern of three adjectives to describe the world. It seems almost as if the world is a 'god' to the speaker - as if (s)he is almost worshipping the world (based on the word 'miraculous'). There is also additional personification here, in the adjectives 'forgiving' and 'maternal'. This links back to the title 'Mother'.

[12] This is a horrible way to describe us: 'we parasites'. The personal pronoun 'we' brings the reader into the poem; as if they are now a part of this 'we parasites'. This is quite shocking and horrible to the reader, to think of him/herself as a parasite. It also changes the meaning of 'host'. We could initially think that 'host' is being used to mean e.g. a party host, i.e. being used in a nice way. However, the link with parasite makes it seem like we are irritating bugs living on a 'host' creature.

[13] The repetition of 'abuses' here reinforces the personification of the earth as a 'mother' - we are not just plundering the earth's natural resources, we are 'abusing' her.

[14] This is where the 'irritations' the speaker talks about become more abstract - it's no longer the 'abuses' we enact on the world (i.e. pollution etc.) that are the issue, but the 'abuses' we enact on one another (i.e. war, intolerance, violence). Referring to all of humankind as 'her children', i.e. children of the world, implies that the speaker is trying to show us that we are all one family and that we shouldn't be treating one another in the negative way that we do sometimes.

[15] Finishing the poem with these two rhetorical questions is quite powerful and poignant. The pattern of three (violence, intolerance, fear) is very strong and hints that the speaker perhaps doesn't believe that the earth's tears can wash them away - it's a very interesting metaphor, because it's both personifying the earth and also turning abstract concepts into physical irritations that could potentially be 'washed away'. The second question then turns the idea on its head and asks whether the earth would actually care in the first place, reminding us that this is all pure speculation. The final three words, though, are quite affecting - 'like we do'. Again, the use of the personal, but inclusive pronoun 'we' ties the reader in with the speaker and adds a sense of guilt to the poem - it implies that we are all complicit in ignoring the problems in our world.

Learning

The choreography
of geography
seems to want to be
enigmatic.

I'm not smart
at art
It's, at heart,
traumatic.

History's
victories
are mysteries
to me.

Let's extinguish
English
and relinquish
it easily.

Systematic
mathematics
is dramatically
tragic.

In defiance
of science
my reliance
is on magic.

I'm spurning
my learning
and yearning
for a rest,

though my elocutionary
vocabulary's
rudimentary
at best

and it's true
that my few
things I knew
have been useful.

Perhaps a few years
more of open ears
wouldn't cause tears
and could be crucial.

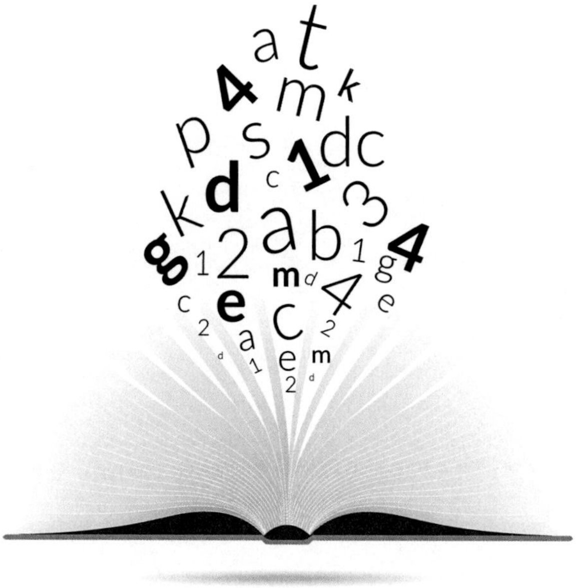

Learning - Annotated

A list poem is exactly what it sounds like – a list. It can be a standard list of items, people or places. It can include lots of repetition or rhyme, but it doesn't have to. Usually a list poem will include some sort of comment on the list – its significance or what it means to the speaker – and might have a twist at the end.

This is a strange rhyme scheme. The rhyme pattern relies on some full and some near rhymes, but as each line is so short, almost the whole line creates the rhyme in most cases, aside from the last stanza. You could discuss with the children what they think this means. Perhaps it's because the final stanza is the most important one. What do they think?

There are some very short lines in this poem. Each stanza seems to have a very similar number of syllables per line, if not exactly the same. You could ask the children what they think this means. Perhaps the speaker is implying that each line is of equal importance. Perhaps (s)he is trying to imply that (s)he doesn't have much to say about these school subjects (although the poem is quite long, which contradicts this idea – maybe this is why the speaker changes his/her mind about the importance of education at the end of the poem).

Line no.	Rhyme scheme	Learning	Syllable Count
1	A	The choreography	6
2	A	of geography	5
3	A	seems to want to be[1]	5
4	B	enigmatic.	4
5	C	I'm not smart	3
6	C	at art	2
7	C	It's, at heart,	3
8	B	traumatic.[2]	3
9	D	History's	3
10	D	victories	3
11	D	are mysteries	4
12	E	to me.	2
13	F	[03] Let's extinguish	4
14	F	[03] English	2
15	F	and relinquish[3]	4
16	E	it easily.	4
17	G	Systematic[4]	4
18	G	mathematics	4
19	G	is dramatically	5
20	H	tragic.[5]	2
21	I	In defiance	4
22	I	of science	3
23	I	my reliance	4
24	H	is on magic.[6]	4
25	J	I'm spurning[7]	3
26	J	my learning	3
27	J	and yearning	3
28	K	for a rest,	3
29	L	though my elocutionary	8
30	L	vocabulary's	5
31	L	rudimentary	5
32	K	at best	2
33	M	and it's true	3
34	M	that my few	3
35	M	things I knew	3
36	N	have been useful.	4
37	O	[8] Perhaps a few years	5
38	O	[8] more of open ears	5
39	O	[8] wouldn't cause tears	4
40	N	and could be crucial.[8]	5

[1] This phrase implies that it's the subject that is being awkward – the speaker has personified 'geography' and made it seem like it is Geography who wants to seem mysterious. What is the effect of this? Perhaps it could be that we, as readers, feel more empathy for the speaker, as it implies that it's not his/her fault that (s)he doesn't understand geography.

[2] This is a strong word to use! This is showing what a bad experience this person has had of the subject – (s)he feels traumatised by it. However, you could argue that this is hyperbole (exaggeration for effect) and that the speaker is trying to make the reader laugh

[3] The words 'extinguish' and 'relinquish' are quite complicated. Is this because the speaker is hinting that, despite how (s)he claims not to be any good at these subjects, (s)he is actually quite good?

[4] Why 'systematic'? Is this a dig at 'the system', i.e. school?

[5] Another strong word – is this more hyperbole?

[6] This is quite funny – (s)he's 'defying' science and relying instead on 'magic'. This is quite a silly thing to say – perhaps this, combined with the hyperbole from lines 20 and 8, this means that the speaker is not taking things quite as seriously as (s)he seems to be

[7] This speaker is strongly rejecting the idea of school and learning. However, this word, linked with 'yearning' has connotations of a love affair. You might 'spurn' someone's proposal or 'spurn' their love, or you might be 'yearning' after the person who has spurned you. Perhaps this is why the words 'spurning' and 'yearning' are linked together by the rhymes on lines 25 and 27. Perhaps the speaker actually secretly loves learning. You could discuss with the children why someone might want to hide the fact that they love to learn.

[8] This final stanza appears to go back on everything said in the first section of the poem. The speaker decides that his/her education is actually 'crucial'. This is amusing, because it reinforces the impression you're given throughout the poem that the speaker does actually enjoy learning, is really pretty clever and is only being silly when (s)he says (s)he doesn't like it and isn't very good..

I Don't Want Heaven

I don't want heaven.
When I die, don't trick me out in little stars;
I shall not make the face of heaven fine.
Not for me the wheeling stars and wandering planets,
somersaulting through the eerie darkness.
I want the warmth of summer rain;
The smell of grass in spring;
I will be everything.
Let the busy worms help me out –
I want my reincarnation by installment plan.
My atoms will infuse the soil;
my particles will dance among the reeling leaves;
you will hear me in the whisper of the waves;
you will feel me on the tickle of the breeze;
and when you do, you'll know
that heaven was too far away –
too far away from you.

I Don't Want Heaven - Annotated

A free verse poem is, in some ways, the easiest type of poetry to write. A free verse poem is a poem that does not rhyme and does not have a regular rhythm.

As a free verse poem does not restrict or prescribe the number of syllables per line, the writer can choose. This means that any line which is particularly long or short has been chosen to be that length for a reason. It might be interesting to ask the children to choose a particularly short or long line and discuss why they think the writer has made it that length. As a whole, the poem has only five particularly short lines (of 5 or 6 syllables) - these appear right at the beginning, right at the end and right in the middle. This gives the poem an interesting shape; it goes from short, to long, back to short, up to long and back to short. You could ask the children why they think this is - could it be that the poem is representative of a person's life? Could it be that the speaker is trying to be persuasive, so they are using the persuasive technique of short sentences, scattered at regular intervals, to persuade the reader that heaven is not a good thing?

Line no .	Rhyme scheme	I Don't Want Heaven	Syllable Count
1	A	I don't want heaven.[1]	5
2	B	When I die, [2]don't trick me out in little stars;	11
3	C	I shall not make the face of heaven fine.[2]	10
4	D	Not for me the wheeling stars and wandering planets,[3]	12
5	E	somersaulting[4] through the eerie[5] darkness.	10
6	F	I want[6] the warmth of[7] summer rain;[8]	8
7	G	The smell of grass in spring;[9]	6
8	G	I will be everything.[10]	6
9	H	Let the busy worms help me out[11]–	8
10	I	I want my reincarnation by installment plan.[12]	13
11	J	[18] My atoms will infuse the soil;[13]	8
12	K	[18] my particles will dance among the reeling leaves;[14]	12
13	L	[18] you will hear me in the whisper of the waves;[15]	11
14	K	you[16] will feel me on the tickle of the breeze;[17]	11
15	M	and when you do, you'll know	6
16	N	that heaven was too far away[18]–	8
17	O	[18] too far away from you.[19]	6

[1] Quite a shocking statement to start this poem with. Four bold words. It's the shortest line in the poem, in terms of syllables. This grabs the reader's attention straight away and makes the reader wonder why the speaker is so adamant.

[2] This is a deliberate misquote from Shakespeare's Romeo and Juliet. Juliet implores the night to
'Give me my Romeo. And when I shall die,
Take him and cut him out in little stars,
And he will make the face of heaven so fine
That all the world will be in love with night
And pay no worship to the garish sun.'
The implication here is that the speaker doesn't feel that (s)he would improve 'the face of Heaven' (i.e. the night sky) by becoming a constellation. The replacement of the word 'cut' with 'trick' is interesting. 'Tricked out' is a slightly disparaging phrase for being dressed in an over-the-top manner or wearing too many accessories. The implication could be that the speaker feels that stars would be too over-the-top for him/her. Why could this be? Perhaps (s)je feels that (s)he wouldn't belong in Heaven? Or perhaps (s)he feels that it's not appropriate for him/her for another reason... You could discuss this with the children.

[3] Repetition of the 'w' sound in the two adjectives on this line, combined with the long vowel sounds of 'ee' (in wheeling) and 'a' (in wandering) emphasizes the vastness and emptiness of space. This helps us to empathise with the speaker, as a vast empty space seems quite a cold and uncomfortable place and the implication is that if Heaven is up above the clouds it must be in space. This is an interesting idea - an over-literalisation of the idea of Heaven as being 'up above'.

[4] The verb 'somersaulting' implies a lack of control – close to 'falling' or 'tumbling' but more dangerous, somehow. This reinforces the message that 'Heaven' is a lonely and cold place, like in the previous line.

[5] Another negative adjective to reinforce the message that 'Heaven' is a lonely and cold place, like in the previous lines.

[6] Here, the poem moves from a negative to a positive. The poem began with 'I don't want' and has now moved to 'I want'.

[7] The noun 'warmth' immediately compares favourably to the cold and lonely descriptions given in the previous four lines.

[8] Why 'summer rain'? As opposed to the summer sun? Is the speaker trying to show that (s) is not asking for too much? Is it because the rain is something which falls from the clouds, so perhaps (s)he is implying (s)he wants to fall back down to earth?

[9] Why in spring? Is (s)he implying that (s)he will come back to the world as a new person? This could be a reference to reincarnation, which would link to line 10. This is also a hint at a long-term arrangement; summer, then the following spring - the speaker intends to come back to the world forever, perhaps?

[10] In terms of number of words, this is the joint shortest line. This gives it a certain status. Why is this? You could discuss this with the children. Potential answers include: it's an equivalent statement to the first line, because it's stating what the speaker WILL be, as opposed to what (s)he DOESN'T want; it's a summary of what the speaker is trying to say; it's a type of oxymoron - the shortness of the line contrasts the the vastness of 'everything'.

[11] The effect of the enjambment here reinforces the idea that the speaker wants to continue (just like the line). (S)he doesn't want to go on anywehre else - (s)he wants to carry on in this life/world.

[12] This is an interesting phrase! What does reincarnation by installment plan actually mean? Linking this to the 'busy worms', is the speaker perhaps hinting that (s)he wants to be buried and become part of the earth in a literal sense as well as a metaphorical sense?

[13] 'infuse' seems like quite a nice verb – as if the 'atoms' are bringing a new flavour and substance to the soil.

[14] 'dance' here links to 'reeling', as a reel is a type of dance. The implication is of joyfulness - the 'particles' are personified in a very happy way, as they're dancing for joy.

[15] The alliteration of 'whisper' and 'wind' make an aural image of the sound of the leaves.

[16] These personal pronouns are interesting: the repetition of 'my', 'my', 'you', 'you', changes from first to second person. This is the first time the reader has been directly addressed. You could ask the children to imagine who the speaker is addressing. Is it a generic 'reader'? Or do they think it's someone specific?

[17] 'Tickle' is an interesting verb to have chosen here. The breeze is being personified as a playful person. Perhaps the speaker's personality is being communicated to some extent here - the speaker is a playful person and wants to 'tickle' the reader, even in the afterlife!

[18] The repetition here is particularly interesting because it is the first proper repetition of a phrase in the poem. The enjambment and the dash link the repeated phrases together quite closely and imply that this is a significant phrase. Why is it significant? Perhaps this gives more clues as to the 'reader' the speaker has in mind. This might imply that the 'you' the speaker is talking to is a specific person. Who could it be? Or it might be that the phrase is repeated because the phrase itself is significant - 'far away'; the speaker might be repeating 'far' because the distance is so great, in his/her imagination.

[19] Finishing the poem with a second person pronoun is a way of showing the significance of the person the speaker is addressing. This could contribute to your discussion of who that person could be with the children.

Galileo

Whenever Galileo
ate tuna mixed with mayo,
he'd curse the vile depravity
of the portions lost to gravity.

The writer here has chosen to use a regular rhythm. Why is that? How does it add to the effect? You could argue that it makes the poem flow more nicely, which means it has a greater impact, when we reach the amusing 'punch line' of a last line.

Line no .	Rhyme scheme	Galileo	Syllable Count
1	A	Whenever Galileo[1]	7
2	A	ate tuna mixed with mayo,	7
3	B	he'd curse[2] the vile depravity[3]	8
4	B	of the portions lost to gravity.[4]	9

[1] A clerihew is a four line poem about a famous person. Every clerihew should begin with the name of the famous person the poem is about as the first line. It can be the whole line, or just most of the line. The rhyme scheme is always AABB and the rhythm is usually fairly regular, but it doesn't have to be. The clerihew ought to gently poke fun at the famous person, in a funny, but not unkind, way. Often a reference to the reason that they're famous is included.

[2] This is a gentle reference to the time in which Galileo was living – a very superstitious time, in which most people believed in devils and angels and curses. Galileo's discoveries were declared heretical, as the Catholic Church refused to believe that the sun didn't go round the earth – they believed that the earth was the centre of the universe, because God had made it so.

[3] This is another word used to describe Galileo's discoveries in the field of astronomy

[4] Although we usually think of Galileo as being primarily an astronomer, he was also one of the first people to prove that gravity acts on two objects in the same way, regardless of their weight (previously, Aristotle had stated that heavier objects fall faster).

On the bust of Shakespeare, Holy Trinity Church, Stratford-upon-Avon

Who's there?

Is it you, dear father of the stage?
I fear not.

The eyes stare woodenly,
as blank as an empty page.

There is no trace of the laughter, the tears,
the life that lives still in your words.

Perhaps it was ever
a foregone conclusion,
that any search for you here would be
a wild goose chase.

This mortal coil must have been
claustrophobic
for a soul like yours.

Is it any wonder
that this
stony-hearted
statue could not tether you?

I imagine your spirit,
swift as a shadow
spiraling up, up, up
and melting into thin air.
To go on
to whatever comes.

Your plays are
such stuff as dreams are made on
and dreams are not carved from stone or wood,
(though they may be created on it).

As single-minded as earth,
your image writes on air,
just as you once spun air castles
with your pen.

For that, if nothing else,
it bears resemblance to you.
For that, then, I agree
all's well that ends well.

On the bust of Shakespeare... - Annotated

Structurally, this is a free verse poem. A free verse poem is, in some ways, the easiest type of poetry to write. A free verse poem is a poem that does not rhyme and does not have a regular rhythm. However, this poem has the added advantage of being a personification poem. The writer has written to the bust of William Shakespeare, but has also personified the bust, as if the bust were the real person.

On the bust of Shakespeare, Holy Trinity Church, Stratford-upon-Avon	Syllable Count
Who's there?[1]	2
Is it you[2], dear father of the stage?[3]	9
I fear not.[4]	3
The eyes stare[5] woodenly,[6]	6
as blank as an empty page.[7]	7
There is no trace of the laughter, the tears,	10
the life that lives still in your[2] words.[8]	8
Perhaps it was ever	6
[11] a foregone conclusion,[9]	6
[11] that any search for you[2] here would be	9
a wild goose chase.[10 11]	4
This mortal coil[12] must have been	7
claustrophobic	4
for a soul like yours.[2]	5
Is it any wonder	6
that this	2
stony-hearted[13 14]	4
statue[14] could not tether you?[2 15]	7
I imagine your[2] spirit,	7
swift as a shadow[16]	5
spiraling up, up, up[17]	6
and melting into thin air.18	7
[19] To go on[16]	3
to whatever comes.[19]	5
Your[2] plays are	3
such stuff as dreams are made on[20]	7
and dreams[21] are not carved from stone or wood,[22]	9
(though they may be created on it).[23]	9
As single-minded as earth,[24]	7
your[2] image writes on air,	6
just as you[2] once spun air castles[25]	8
with your[2] pen.	3
[26] For that, if nothing else,	6
it bears resemblance to you.[2 26]	7
For that, then, I agree	6
all's well that ends well.[27]	5

[1] This is the way in which Shakespeare starts one of his most famous plays: Hamlet. It is a fantastic opening for a play, because it immediately allows the audience to know the setting, the mood and the characters: it's dark, someone is anxious (why? We are shortly to find out), and immediately the question is answered, so we know who the characters are. Starting the poem like this is clever on the part of the poet, because it's a quote, but it's also a question posed to the bust: who is there? It sets up the personification, the Shakespearean references and the questioning of the speaker (who continues to speculate and wonder throughout the poem, as to the life and death of William Shakespeare).

[2] The speaker is speaking directly to the bust of Shakespeare, but as if (s)he is speaking to him directly. This is an extended piece of personification throughout the poem.

[3] Another question. This is a rhetorical question, as the bust obviously cannot answer. However, its tone is interesting: 'dear father of the stage' is both very familiar (dear father) and very formal (father of the stage). There is a juxtaposition here. Many people feel that they 'know' a writer or an actor based on reading or seeing their work, so perhaps the speaker is implying that due to reading Shakespeare's plays (s)he feels like they have a relationship, but by calling him 'father of the stage' (s)he is also showing that (s)he knows they really don't. This might be a good opportunity to discuss the difference between a writer and a speaker in a poem – perhaps the writer acknowledges that the speaker and Shakespeare don't have the close relationship that the speaker seems to hint at (hence the juxtaposition, between the speaker's point of view and the writer's point of view). Father of the stage is an interesting phrase, also.

[4] 'Fear' is a strong verb here. Why does the speaker 'fear' that Shakespeare is not really here? Perhaps because the speaker has come to see him and is sad that the experience is disappointing. Perhaps because the speaker is doubting the physical likeness between the real Shakespeare and the bust.

[5] This is personification, because the 'eyes' are actually not real.

[6] There is a double entendre here; there is both the meaning of inexpressively or stiffly and also the reference to the fact that the bust is not a real person (although it's made of stone, not wood – perhaps the 'wood' could refer to the stage Shakespeare worked on).

On the bust of Shakespeare... - Annotated

[7] The simile here is interesting, because it has reference to 'an empty page', which is, of course, what Shakespeare would have written on to create his masterpieces.

[8] Personification of 'words' as a living being.

[9] 'Foregone conclusion' is a phrase invented by Shakespeare in the play 'Othello'. (For the purposes of these annotations, I will say that Shakespeare invented this and other quotes - in actual fact, we are not sure as to whether he invented them or whether he was the first person to put them in writing for posterity.)

[10] 'Wild goose chase' is a phrase invented by Shakespeare in the play 'Romeo and Juliet'.

[11] Why was it a 'foregone conclusion' that the speaker wouldn't find Shakespeare here? Physically, he is at the church, or rather his bones are (he's buried there), but spiritually, the speaker seems to think it's obvious he wouldn't be. You could discuss why this might be. Perhaps it's because his spirit would be more likely to haunt somewhere like the Globe, where he spent most of his time. Perhaps it's because his spirit would be in heaven.

[12] 'Shuffle off this mortal coil' is a phrase invented by Shakespeare in the play 'Hamlet'. It means 'to die'. So 'mortal coil' means the world. The speaker is implying that the world was too 'claustrophobic' for Shakespeare. Why would this be? Perhaps the implication here is that Shakespeare's spirit was too great/large for this world (maybe because he was a genius, in the eyes of the speaker at least).

[13] 'Stony-hearted villain' is a phrase invented by Shakespeare in Henry IV Part I

[14] The statue/bust is being personified as 'stony-hearted' here, but there is also a double entendre on the word 'stony', as the statue is literally made of stone.

[15] This is a rhetorical question, designed to imply how obvious it is, in a way, that Shakespeare's spirit would not be in the bust.

[16] 'Swift as a shadow' is a phrase (a simile, in fact) invented by Shakespeare in 'A Midsummer Night's Dream'.

[17] The repetition of one word three times is a technique known as epizeuxis. It is effective here, because it shows the progress of Shakespeare's spirit to heaven. The repetition could be said to show how far the spirit has to travel, or perhaps to show the manner of travel, as though the spirit is travelling on the wind and being blown like a feather, up a bit, down, around, then up again.

[18] 'Vanishing into thin air' is a phrase that was invented by Shakespeare in 'The Tempest'.

[19] This is a short phrase with mostly monosyllabic words, but it has strong implications for what the speaker imagines has happened to Shakespeare. Shakespeare's plays are full of imagery about heaven and the afterlife and religion. This phrase shows that the speaker is joining that speculation.

[20] 'We are such stuff as dreams are made on' is a phrase invented by Shakespeare in 'The Tempest'

[21] The repetition of 'dreams' reinforces the idea that Shakespeare's plays are dreamlike, aspirational perhaps - certainly that they spark their imagination.

[22] You could link this to the reference to the bust's eyes staring 'woodenly'

[23] This is a reference to the fact that Shakespeae 'created dreams' on a stage made from 'wood'.

[24] Another simile. The speaker constantly refers to dreams and spirits and has now come 'down to earth'. The 'image' (or bust) could be said to be single-minded because it is frozen in the attitude in which is was created.

[25] We're back to heavenly imagery here, or dream-like imagery, instead of 'earth'. This metaphor shows, again, the speaker's respect for Shakespeare's writing.

[26] The speaker changes his/her point of view here slightly - (s)he has initially been stating his/her disappointment with the bust, but now changes to say that the bust does actually represent something about Shakespeare accurately.

[27] All's Well That Ends Well is the title of a play written by Shakespeare. It's also a remarkably succinct way to end the poem; you could say that it's implying that the poem is 'ending well' because it's ending with a quote from Shakespeare! Or it could be a reference to the speaker's experience of seeing the Shakespeare bust. It started poorly, because of his/her disappointment that his spirit wasn't reflected in the stone face, but it ended well because (s)he approved of the way he is holding his pen in the air.

The Ballad of Alexander Fleming

If you ask 'what makes a hero?'
you'll get many a response.
Mostly detailing heroic wars
remembered now in songs.

But what else is a hero,
but a person who saves lives?
If that's the definition,
our subject surely qualifies.

Alexander Fleming
was a Scotsman, born and bred.
He worked in shipping first,
then turned to medicine instead.

Conscientiously, he researched
injury care in the war
and in 1918 he came home,
to research, as before,

in London. All his war research
was what he worked on then.
To try to stop wounds causing death
for all those brave young men.

In 1921, he made
his first discovery.
Lysozyme – it's a natural
antiseptic. Victory!

But Alexander didn't stop
to praise his cleverness.
He carried on and upped the game
of his inventiveness.

In 1928, while on
a mission to create
a stronger way to kill germs
and heal at a faster rate,

he stopped and looked and rubbed his eyes
and famously exclaimed
'That's funny!' and, from those two words,
Sir. Fleming made his name.

What Fleming found so funny
was his bacteria was gone.
A culture he'd been growing
had a funny fungus on.

Where fungus grew, bacteria died.
That seemed the simple rule.
So now, to find out why and how
was his next job to do.

On the heels of his discovery,
a very thorough team did
lots of work to find the substance
in the fungus that they needed.

Their names were Howard Florey
and Ernst Chain: a super team.
They made the first pure penicillin
there had ever been.

Florey, Chain and Fleming
shared the famous Nobel Prize.
Have three men ever saved
so many millions of lives?

Although many discoveries
were made before and after,
it's hard to think of any
that had an impact faster.

They started mass production
of the drug in '41.
By 1944 they could treat
every last person

wounded at the D-Day landings
in the June of that year.
Its usefulness in fighting disease
soon became quite clear.

In conclusion, dear old Fleming
(aided by Florey and Chain)
saved the lives of countless people
and we can't forget his name,

for he is the type of person
we should all aspire to be.
Perhaps you will be too one day.
We'll have to wait and see.

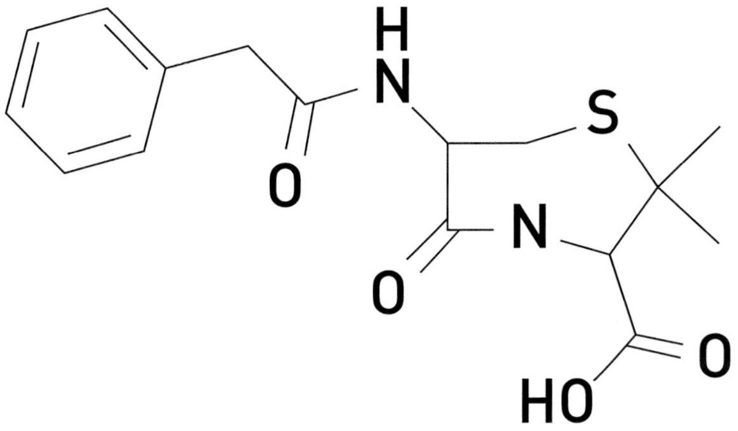

The Ballad of Alexander Fleming - Annotated

A ballad is a poem which tells a story. It is usually a love story, but not always. Ballads date back thousands of years and, in their earliest forms, were usually designed to be sung. For this reason, they have a fairly regular rhythm and a very regular rhyme scheme. The rhyme scheme is usually abXb, where X is a choice: it can rhyme with 'a' or it can not. Ballads are usually composed of four-line stanzas.

The rhythm is fairly regular, to fit the song-like or chant-like ethos of the poem, so you can see that the number of syllables on each line are generally very similar. One thing you could do with the children is spot any particularly long or short lines and consider why they might be so short/long. Is there a particularly important message that needed to be given in that line?

Line no .	Rhyme scheme	Syllable Count	The Ballad of Alexander Fleming
1	A	8	If you ask 'what makes a hero?'
2	B	7	you'll get many a response.
3	C	9	Mostly detailing heroic[1] wars
4	B	6	remembered now in songs.
5	D	7	[2] But what else is a hero[1],
6	E	7	but a person who saves lives?[2]
7	F	7	If that's the definition,
8	E	8	our subject surely[3] qualifies.
9	G	6	Alexander Fleming[4]
10	H	7	was a Scotsman, born and bred.
11	I	6	He worked in shipping first,
12	H	8	then turned to medicine instead.
13	J	8	Conscientiously[5], he researched
14	K	7	injury care in the war
15	L	9	and in 1918 he came home,
16	K	6	[6] to research, as before,
17	M	8	in London. All his war research[6]
18	N	6	was what he worked on then.
19	O	8	To try to stop wounds causing death
20	N	6	for all those brave young men.
21	P	8	In 1921, he made
22	Q	6	his first[7] discovery.
23	R	7	Lysozyme - it's a natural
24	Q	7	antiseptic. Victory![8]
25	S	8	But Alexander didn't stop
26	T	6	to praise his cleverness.
27	U	8	He carried on and upped the game[9]
28	T	6	of his inventiveness.
29	V	8	In 1928, while on
30	W	6	a mission[10] to create
31	X	7	a stronger way to kill germs
32	W	7	and heal at a faster rate,
33	Y	8	he stopped and looked and rubbed his eyes[11]
34	Z	6	and famously exclaimed
35	AA	8	'That's funny!'[12] and, from those two words,
36	Z	6	Sir. Fleming made his name.
37	BB	7	What Fleming found so funny

[1] Repetition of 'hero/heroic' to reinforce the message that Alexander Fleming is a hero.

[2] Rhetorical question: persuasive.

[3] Persuasive adverb

[4] Subject gets his own line for his name: the start of a stanza. Shows his importance

[5] Adverb. Praise for Fleming.

[6] Enjambment: the stanza's are closely linked. This reinforces the idea that Fleming continued his work – he carried on, just like the poem/story does.

[7] The adjective 'first' implies that there will be more to come. The most important (i.e. penicillin) is yet to come. This is a 'teaser' for the big event later!

[8] One word sentence and exclamation mark: provides emphasis and shows how important this discovery was.

[9] This metaphor (you could argue it's a cliché) makes Fleming seem more human and relatable.

[10] Strong noun (hyperbole) to show Fleming's dedication and hard-working attitude

[11] Pattern of three, plus repetition of 'and' makes this a long and rhythmic line...this is to highlight that this is the point at which Fleming is making his big discovery.

[12] This is, apparently, what Fleming actually said when he noticed that a fungus was killing off the bacteria.

Line no .	Rhyme scheme	Syllable Count	The Ballad of Alexander Fleming
38	CC	7	was bacteria was gone.
39	DD	7	A culture he'd been growing
40	CC	7	had a funny fungus[13] on.
41	EE	8	Where fungus grew, bacteria died.
42	FF	6	That seemed the simple rule.
43	GG	8	So now, to find out why and how
44	FF	6	was his next job to do.
45	HH	9	On the heels of his discovery[14],
46	II	7	a very thorough team did
47	JJ	8	lots of work to find the substance
48	II	8	in the fungus that they needed.
49	KK	7	Their names were Howard Florey
50	LL	7	and Ernst Chain: a super team.
51	MM	9	They made the first pure penicillin[15]
52	LL	5	there had ever been.
53	NN	6	Florey, Chain and Fleming
54	OO	7	shared the famous Nobel Prize.
55	PP	6	Have three men ever saved
56	OO	8	so many millions of lives?[16]
57	QQ	8	Although many discoveries
58	RR	7	were made before and after,
59	SS	7	it's hard to think of any
60	RR	7	that had an impact faster.[17]
61	TT	7	They started mass production
62	UU	7	of the drug in '41.
63	VV	9	By 1944 they could treat
64	UU	5	every last person
65	WW	8	wounded at the D-Day landings
66	XX	6	in the June of that year.
67	YY	9	Its usefulness in fighting sickness
68	XX	5	soon became quite clear.
69	ZZ	8	In conclusion, dear old[18] Fleming
70	AAA	7	(aided by Florey and Chain)
71	BBB	8	saved the lives of countless[19] people
72	AAA	7	and we should revere[20] his name,
73	CCC	8	for he is the type of person
74	DDD	7	we should all aspire to be.
75	EEE	8	Perhaps you will be too one day.
76	DDD	6	We'll have to wait and see.[21]

[13] Alliteration; draws attention to the word 'fungus' which is the important word, but also makes it seem slightly comical.

[14] Metaphor; makes it seem like it was all happening very quickly.

[15] Technically accurate, but also alliteration.

[16] LINK to line 55 as well. Rhetorical question for emphasis.

[17] LINK to lines 57, 58, 59. This whole stanza simply praises the importance of the discovery. The phrase 'hard to think of' is a generous one: it allows the possibility that there are other very important discoveries, but still repeats the idea that Fleming's is the best!

[18] Quite informal; makes him sound like a relative or a friend – more human and real.

[19] Possibly hyperbole – although you could argue that this adjective is actually accurate: we couldn't put an accurate figure on the number of lives penicillin has saved.

[20] Also, possibly hyperbole. Is 'revere' too strong a word? Or is it a metaphor? Either way, it goes to show the strength of feeling as to how impressive Fleming's discovery really was.

[21] LINK to line 75 as well. Personal second person pronouns: the poem finishes with a direct address to the reader, bringing the reader into the poem and giving a clear message to them about the usefulness and importance of Fleming's discovery and potential future discoveries.

UN Convention on the Rights of the Child: Rap

Tap your feet
to the beat.
Take a seat,
I'll keep it sweet,
but there is something you need
to find out, yes indeed,
it's your right,
and you might
need to look to the light
of the law.
It's the law.

At the end of the last century,
some governments met
to decide what sort of rights
every last child should get.
Every child in this country
gets these rights, no matter what.
It doesn't matter who their god is
or what money they've got.

Tap your feet
to the beat.
Take a seat,
I'll keep it sweet,
but there is something you need
to find out, yes indeed,
it's your right,
and you might
need to look to the light
of the law.
It's the law.

As a child of this country,
you have rights of your own,
like the rights to live, be cared for
and to have a safe home.
You've the right to have your own name
and to go to school for free.
You don't have to be employed
the way some children must be.

Tap your feet
to the beat.
Take a seat,
I'll keep it sweet,
but there is something you need
to find out, yes indeed,
it's your right,
and you might
need to look to the light
of the law.
It's the law.

You have the right to be protected
from bad people out there.
You have the right to be patched up
with the best medical care.
You have the right to have enough
to eat and plenty to drink.
You have the right to make good friends
and to say what you think.

Take some time
for this rhyme
to sink in.
Have a grin.
You have rights
and the night's
not so lonely
when you're only
one small pace
from a face
that can help.

Right then, now you know your rights
you will be more confident
to feel supported by the
British government.
Don't forget though that you're lucky:
many countries exist
who said they would not award these rights.
Be grateful yours did.

Tap your feet
to the beat.
Take a seat,
I'll keep it sweet,
but there is something you need
to find out, yes indeed,
it's your right,
and you might
need to look to the light
of the law.
It's the law.

UN Convention on the Rights of the Child: Rap - Annotated

A rap is usually defined as 'a series of rhyming lyrics that are spoken or chanted, usually with musical accompaniment'. A nice way to explore this rap (or any the children write in class) might be to give the children different pieces of music and get them to choose which is the most appropriate to rap to. The origins of rap date back to 1960s Jamaica and rap formed an integral part of the hip hop scene of 1970s New York (this could be an interesting research project). Rap is characterized by repetition, short lines, rhythmic, rhyming stanzas and, usually, a chorus and a bridge.

You will note that the number of syllables is very regular. The chorus, naturally, is repeated, so the pattern of syllables repeats too, but throughout the poem, the number of syllables in each corresponding line of each verse is very similar. Rap tends to be based on very similar line lengths, to keep the rapper able to fit the words to the beat.

Line no.	Rhyme scheme	UN Convention on the Rights of the Child: Rap	Syllable Count
1	A	[5]Tap your feet	3
2	A	[5]to the beat.	3
3	A	[5]Take a seat,	3
4	A	[5]I'll keep it sweet,[1]	4
5	B	[5]but there is something[2] you need	7
6	B	[5]to find out, yes indeed,	6
7	C	[5]it's your right,	3
8	C	[5]and you might	3
9	C	[5]need[03] to look to the light[4]	6
10	D	[5]of the law.	3
11	D	[5]It's the law.[6]	3
12	E	At the end of the last century,[7]	9
13	F	some governments met	5
14	G	to decide what sort of rights	7
15	F	every last child should get.	7
16	H	Every child in this country	7
17	I	[08]gets these rights, no matter what.	7
18	J	[08]It doesn't matter who their god is	9
19	I	or what money they've got.[8]	6
20	K	Tap your feet	3
21	K	to the beat.	3
22	K	Take a seat,	3
23	K	I'll keep it sweet,	4
24	L	but there is something you need	7
25	L	to find out, yes indeed,	6
26	M	it's your right,	3
27	M	and you might	3
28	M	need to look to the light	6
29	N	of the law.	3
30	N	It's the law.	3
31	O	As a child of this country,	7
32	P	you have rights of your own,	6
33	Q	[11]like the rights to live, be cared for	8
34	P	[11]and to have a safe home.	6
35	R	[11]You've the right to have your own name[9]	8
36	S	[11]and to go to school for free.[10]	7
37	T	[11]You don't have to be employed	7
38	S	the way some children must be.[11]	7
39	U	Tap your feet	3
40	U	to the beat.	3

[1] Interesting use of colloquialism here. 'Keep it sweet', meaning 'keep it short and to the point'. Raps do tend to be quite colloquial. Children tend to use a lot of colloquialisms too, so perhaps you could argue that this is a way of the speaker showing that (s)he is taking account of his/her audience.

[2] 'Something' is quite a loose word – it doesn't give you any kind of information – it's a teasing word. This could be a way of getting the reader to feel curious and interested in what the 'something' could be.

[3] This is a strong verb: not just 'choose' or 'want' but 'need'. Why might one 'need' to look to the law? You could discuss this with the children. Perhaps it's because the law is the ultimate in protection – it's what is supposed to keep us all safe – so we don't necessarily 'want' to have to invoke the law, but sometimes we need to.

[4] What do you think the speaker means by this? The alliteration of 'look', 'light' and 'law' indicates that this might be a significant phrase – perhaps the 'law' is something that sheds 'light' on dark situations? Perhaps it's the proverbial 'shining beacon' that we should be holding up as an example.

[5] The poem begins with the chorus. This is repeated a further three times throughout the poem. This provides a linking thread throughout the poem, referring back to the importance of the children's rights and encouraging them to pay attention.

[6] The repetition of the final line of this chorus gives a certain importance to it. It makes it seem like nobody can disagree with what the speaker is trying to say, because 'it's the law' – it's unarguable with!

[7] The first line of this stanza changes the rhythm completely. Perhaps practice this out loud with the children – how would they say it? This is usual with raps – quite often the chorus and the verses have different rhythms.

[8] These two lines indicate that circumstances don't matter when it comes to having rights. You could discuss with the children what other classifications there are that they might think would exclude them from receiving the same treatment as their peers – to make the point that these rights are universal. You could also discuss why these two are the ones the speaker has chosen to mention. Are they the most important? If so, why? If not, why not? Perhaps it's more about perception - people think that these are the be all and end all of what makes a person sometimes, but clearly that is not the case.

UN Convention on the Rights of the Child: Rap - Annotated

Line no.	Rhyme scheme	UN Convention on the Rights of the Child: Rap	Syllable Count
41	U	Take a seat,	3
42	U	I'll keep it sweet,	4
43	V	but there is something you need	7
44	V	to find out, yes indeed,	6
45	W	it's your right,	3
46	W	and you might	3
47	W	need to look to the light	6
48	X	of the law.	3
49	X	It's the law.	3
50	Y	You have the right to be protected	9
51	Z	from bad people out there.	6
52	AA	You have the right to be patched up[12]	8
53	Z	with the best medical care.	7
54	BB	You have the right to have enough	8
55	CC	to eat and plenty to drink.	7
56	DD	You have the right to make good friends	8
57	CC	and to say what you think.[13]	6
58	EE	Take some time	3
59	EE	for this rhyme	3
60	FF	to sink in.	3
61	FF	[15]Have a grin.	3
62	GG	[15]You have rights	3
63	GG	[15]and the night's	3
64	HH	[15]not so lonely	4
65	HH	[15]when you're only	4
66	II	[15]one small pace	3
67	II	[15]from a face[14]	3
68	JJ	that can help.[15]	3
69	KK	Right then, now you know your rights	7
70	LL	you will be more confident	7
71	MM	to feel supported by the	7
72	LL	good old British government.[16]	7
73	NN	Don't forget though that you're lucky:	8
74	OO	many countries exist	6
75	PP	who said that they would not award[17] these rights.	10
76	OO	Be grateful yours did.[18]	5
77	QQ	Tap your feet	3
78	QQ	to the beat.	3
79	QQ	Take a seat,	3
80	QQ	I'll keep it sweet.	4
81	RR	but there is something you need	7
82	RR	to find out, yes indeed,	6
83	SS	it's your right,	3
84	SS	and you might	3
85	SS	need to look to the light	6
86	TT	of the law.	3
87	TT	It's the law.[19]	3

[9] This might be a good discussion point for the children – you could link it to the Romans, who often named their children with numerical names, because the death rate was so high and because aristocratic Romans were rather removed from family life, so their children were basically called 'first', 'second', 'third'. How would it make us feel these days if we were given these sorts of names? Perhaps you could discuss what it means to have your own name...bring in, for example, the history of slavery and how slaves names would be taken away from them and they would be given their masters surnames to show ownership.

[10] Another interesting discussion point – why is it so significant that we have free education in this country? You could discuss the history of education and when education became free and necessary in this country. You could discuss countries where education is still not a right for all or parts of the populations (perhaps discuss Malala Yousafzai).

[11] This section details some of the rights given to children under the UN Convention of the Rights of the Child. It might be worth mentioning to the children that this only happened in 1989. That's within the lifetimes of most of their parents (to give it some context). You could discuss these rights with the children. The poem focuses initially on the most basic ones (to live, to be safe) and moves up to e.g. go to school for free and not be allowed to work. You could discuss with the children what other rights they have and what rights they think they should have. You could also turn it on its head and disucss the responsibilities that go along with these rights.

[12] Some more colloquial language here. This keeps the tone light and friendly, while still imparting plenty of information.

[13] This is quite a simple phrase, but it carries a huge amount of importance – it might be worth discussing this with the children. The one-syllable words are deceptively simple and create a juxtaposition with the importance of the information within it.

[14] Why 'face'? This is an example of synecdoche, where a part of something is used to refer to the whole thing (face instead of person). So why has the poet chosen to do this? Perhaps because the face is the friendliest part of a person and the poet is trying to show that there are friendly and helpful people whose job it is to help children if their rights are being compromised.

[15] This is the bridge – the section that moves the poem/rap/song on to its concluding sections. The bridge usually is a reflective piece, so, here, the speaker is asking the reader to reflect on what the poem has told the reader so far. It's drawing a conclusion from the information so far on behalf of the reader: 'the night's not so lonely when you're only one small pace from a face that can help'. The conclusion is, perhaps, that the reader should feel reassured and comforted by the fact that the law is there as a protection and that children don't have to feel alone because there are people out there who can help.

[16] A colloquial description of the government as the 'good old' British government. This implies that the government are friendly; they are being described in terms that you would use for a dear friend who you've known for years and is reliable. This phrase carries connotations of trust and safety.

[17] Interesting choice of verb. Why 'award'? You could discuss with the children whether these rights are something innate or something which can be given. The poet might be implying here that the children should be grateful (as in line 76) because not everyone has these rights. This is a subtle hint that although we call these conditions 'rights', actually, they are not a natural thing, they are a societal thing which we have created and we have to be careful to protect them, and also fulfill our societal responsibilities, to protect the society which has allowed us these rights.

[18] It could be argued that this is the overall message of the poem: it's teaching children not only what their rights are, but also that they should be grateful for the support they receive, as laid down in law, by the government.

[19] The repetition of 'the law' in the final two lines of this poem complete the thematic string which begins in the first chorus and continues throughout the poem, every time the chorus occurs. It is a way of 'bookending' the poem and providing a summative conclusion.

The Man

1. Watery eyes see clearly fifty years ago.
2. The bed of creases envelops his ancient smile,
telling stories of youthful
3. laughter, long since gone.
4. An overgrown forest hides his secrets.

The Man - Annotated

This is an image poem. Image poems are really good ones to encourage the children to write, because you can be as supportive or as flexible as you feel the children need you to be and there is a simple start point for them to begin collating ideas. In brief, the children use a high quality image and write about it. However, they can use it in the sense of a very vague startpoint – 'tell me what this makes you think of' – or you can create a really specific set of criteria about the image – 'pick five features that you can see within the poem and use word association to come up with ten words which relate to each one...etc.' The poem can be super short or as long as the children (and/or you) want it to be. The idea of an image poem is to make children think really hard about their word choice. Does that adjective fully describe the real 'blueness' of the water? Does that verb fully portray the massive strength of the bird, if it should choose to move?

Line no.	The Man	Syllable Count[1]
1	Watery eyes[2] see clearly[3] fifty years ago.	12
2	The bed of creases[4] envelops his ancient smile, telling stories of youthful	19
3	laughter, long since gone.	5
4	An overgrown forest hides his secrets.[5]	10

[1] The structure of the poem is quite irregular. Why do the children think this is? Could it be because the old man's face is quite irregular – wrinkled and pitted with age? Could it be because his life has been irregular and that's why he has (as it says on line 4) 'secrets'?

[2] Why are the man's eyes watery? This could be to do with his age, but it could also be referring to the emotions he is feeling. Is he getting emotional and upset, thinking about the past? Why could that be? You could discuss this with the children – what would make someone regretful?

[3] This adverb is interesting – do the 'watery' eyes see clearer in the past? Why? Is this an 'age' thing or is the man remembering something specific? Look again at the image – what emotions do the children think the man is experiencing at this present time?

[4] What do the children think this could be referring to? Perhaps it's a metaphor for the wrinkles around the man's mouth? Perhaps it's referring to an actual bed, in which he might sleep...or even die. It could mean both of these. The next line could be extending the metaphor of the wrinkles around his mouth, by saying that they were caused by 'laughter, long since gone'. Or perhaps it is referring to the idea of people (probably family) gathering at the old man's bedside as he tells them 'stories of laughter'.

[5] What do the children think of this line? It could be a metaphor for the man's moustache – perhaps the moustache is 'hiding' his mouth and preventing him from telling his secrets (this could serve to back up the theory that the previous lines are a metaphor for his wrinkles around his mouth). Or perhaps the hair peeking out of his hat is a hint at the 'overgrown forest', and it is therefore his hair that is hiding the secrets inside his mind. Perhaps it's a literal forest, which prevents people visiting him. Or perhaps it's a literal forest that has a house or something in that metaphorically 'hides his secrets'.

There is no frigate like a book
To take us lands away,
Nor any coursers like a page
Of prancing poetry.
This traverse may the poorest take
Without oppress of toll;
How frugal is the chariot
That bears a human soul!

A Book, by Emily Dickinson - Annotated

Line no.	Rhyme scheme	A Book, by Emily Dickinson[1]	Syllable Count[2]
1	A	There is no frigate[3] like a book[4]	8
2	B	[4] To take us lands away,	6
3	C	Nor any coursers[5] like a page	8
4	B	Of prancing poetry.[6]	6
5	D	This traverse[7] may the poorest[8] take	8
6	E	Without oppress of toll;	6
7	F	How frugal is the chariot[9]	8
8	E	That bears a human soul![10]	6

[1] Emily Dickinson (1830-1855) was an American poet. She wrote almost 1800 poems during her life but published hardly any. A lot of her poetry focuses on the beauty of the world around her – the magic of the everyday miracle.

[2] Most of Dickinson's poetry is written in 'ballad stanza', which is composed of quatrains (four line sections) of alternating iambic tetrameter and trimeter. This means that, as you can see, the odd numbered lines have eight syllables and the even numbered lines have six. You can then further break the lines down into metrical feet. A metrical foot in poetry is like a bar in music – it is how we separate rhythmic phrases of the same length. There are four metrical feet (called iambs) in tetrameter and three in trimeter. Each iamb is a unit of rhythm which goes 'da-DUM'. Thus, a line of iambic pentameter goes 'da-DUM da-DUM da-DUM da-DUM da-DUM', where each 'da' and 'DUM' is one syllable. A word such as 'away' has a natural iambic rhythm, because we put the emphasis on the 'way' when we pronounce it, we wouldn't say 'A-way', we would say 'a-WAY'. If you emphasise the natural rhythm of speech when you read a poem composed in iambic meter, you will notice the iambic rhythm immediately.

[3] A frigate is a ship. Interestingly, it's actually a warship, which immediately sets up the imaginative, slightly surreal tone of the poem, showing the power of the imagination and the wonder that can be found in reading, because a frigate is the sort of 'setting' you might find in a novel,

[4] This wonderful image sets up the subject of the poem. The poem talks about how reading books is the easiest, cheapest and most wonderful way to travel and experience the world.

[5] Coursers are horses – they are strong, fast horses which were often used as warhorses during the Middle Ages by knights. This is another reference (like the frigate) to an imaginative, story-like setting, like you would find in a book.

[6] I have called this a rhyme in the rhyme scheme column. Technically speaking it is a near rhyme or half rhyme. There is no need to mispronounce either of the words in an attempt to make them rhyme 'properly'. There is enough similarity between the sounds that they naturally link if you say them the way you normally would.

[7] A traverse is a journey, which Dickinson is saying a book can take you on.

[8] These references to how cheap a hobby reading is show that Dickinson is implying that there is no social barrier to learning or imagining. There is something aspirational about this - and inspirational too. The message is that reading is for everyone.

[9] This metaphor is another reference to a wonderful 'setting' that could be found in a novel; the 'chariot' of a book that can take you on your 'traverse' is a deliberately ancient reference, as chariot is an archaic word. It could be a reference to the Bible, as chariots are often used in Bible stories (and Dickinson was a religious person) but could also be interpreted as a reference to the Romans or other ancient cultures whose stories and poetry still surivive.

[10] This reference to the soul shows that Dickinson is implying that there is an almost religious or spiritual experience to be had through reading. Dickinson was a very religious person and there are often religious images to be found in her poetry.

First autumn morning:
the mirror I stare into
shows my father's face.

Unnamed Haiku, Murakami Kijo - Annotated

Line no.		Syllable Count[1]
1	First autumn[2] morning:[3]	5
2	the mirror I stare[4] into	7
3	shows my father's face.[5]	5

[1] A haiku is a traditional Japanese poem, based on a specific number of syllables per line. The first and third lines have five syllables and the second line has seven. Sometimes poets write haiku chains, i.e. a series of haikus on the same or related subjects.

[2] There is a deliberate double entendre here. As well as it literally being autumn, the poet is implying that he may be in the 'autumn' of his life. You could discuss with the children what the speaker might mean by that.

[3] There is an interesting juxtaposition here, between the 'autumn' and the 'morning'. Morning implies early, fresh, new. Autumn implies a winding down, heading to winter, getting cold. Perhaps the implication is that the speaker's feeling of getting old and becoming his father is something new?

[4] Why is the speaker 'staring' into the mirror? Is this implying that the speaker is feeling a bit down? Perhaps he is feeling a bit old, hence the reference to his father in the final line.

[5] The speaker is using a metaphor here to show that he feels like he is beginning to look just like his father. This, combined with the reference to 'autumn' implies that perhaps he is feeling old. There is a melancholy tone to the poem. You could discuss with the children how the tone is created and why the speaker might feel down upon realising that he looks like his father.

Invictus, by William Ernest Henley

Out of the night that covers me,
Black as the Pit from pole to pole,
I thank whatever gods may be
For my unconquerable soul.

In the fell clutch of circumstance
I have not winced nor cried aloud.
Under the bludgeonings of chance
My head is bloody, but unbowed.

Beyond this place of wrath and tears
Looms but the Horror of the shade,
And yet the menace of the years
Finds, and shall find, me unafraid.

It matters not how strait the gate,
How charged with punishments the scroll.
I am the master of my fate:
I am the captain of my soul.

Line no.	Rhyme scheme[1]	Invictus,[2] by William Ernest Henley[3]	Syllable Count[4]
1	A	Out of the night[5] that covers6 me,	8
2	B	Black as the Pit[7] from pole to pole,[8]	8
3	A	I thank whatever gods may be[9]	8
4	B	For my unconquerable[10] soul.	8
5	C	In the fell clutch[11] of circumstance	8
6	D	I have not winced nor cried aloud.[12]	8
7	C	Under the bludgeonings of chance[13 14]	8
8	D	My head is bloody, but unbowed.[15]	8
9	E	Beyond this place of wrath and tears[16]	8
10	F	Looms but the Horror of the shade,	8
11	E	And yet the menace of the years[17]	8
12	F	Finds, and shall find, me unafraid.	8
13	G	It matters not how strait[18] the gate[19],	8
14	H	How charged with punishments the scroll.[20]	8
15	G	[21] I am the master of my fate:	8
16	H	I am the captain of my soul.[21]	8

[1] The poem has a regular rhyme scheme, which, along with the steady rhythm, helps it feel lyrical – almost like a song.

[2] The poem's title is the Latin word for invincible or unconquerable (as in line 4).

[3] William Ernest Henley was an English poet, critic and editor. This is his most famous poem. He was a humanist and a very influential person in his day, being friends with such characters as Robert Louis Stevenson and J. M. Barrie. From the age of 12, he suffered from tuberculosis of the bone. His life-long struggle with this led to several poems on a similar theme to Invictus – about the strength of one's soul and the importance of fighting against obstacles.

[4] The poem is written in iambic tetrameter. This means that each line has eight syllables, which can be further broken down into four metrical feet. A metrical foot in poetry is like a bar in music – it is how we separate rhythmic phrases of the same length. There are four metrical feet (called iambs) in iambic tetrameter. Each iamb is a unit of rhythm which goes 'da-DUM'. Thus, a line of iambic pentameter goes 'da-DUM da-DUM da-DUM da-DUM da-DUM', where each 'da' and 'DUM' is one syllable. A word such as 'away' has a natural iambic rhythm, because we put the emphasis on the 'way' when we pronounce it, we wouldn't say 'A-way', we would say 'a-WAY'. If you emphasise the natural rhythm of speech when you read a poem composed in iambic meter, you will notice the iambic rhythm immediately.

[5] The 'night' to which the speaker is referring seems to be a metaphorical night, meaning struggle and difficulty.

[6] A verb implying that the speaker can't see any way out – (s)he is entirely enclosed by the difficulties (s)he is in.

[7] This simile refers to the 'Pit' with a capital letter, meaning that the speaker is referring to Hell. In the Victorian era, anything to do with God or the Devil had to be capitalised.

[8] This links to the verb 'covers' in the previous line, implying that the darkness stretches from the North to the South pole, i.e. covers the whole world.

[9] This is a very spiritual poem, as there are several references to the soul and the afterlife. However, it is by no means a religious poem. Henley was a humanist – he did not believe in any organised religion, believing instead that science was the way to understand the world and that people were in charge of thinking for themselves about what is right and wrong, based on respect for others and the use of reasoning. This poem clearly shows that Henley believes that he is charge of his own life and his soul is, in a manner of speaking, his own business. The phrase 'whatever gods may be' is a clear indication that the speaker is not only refusing to accept any one religion, but is doubting the existence of gods at all. The modal verb 'may' shows that he is questioning. Perhaps you could argue that there is a slightly sarcastic tone in this line, with the 'whatever' linked to the 'may'.

[10] This is a reference back to the title of the poem: Invictus is Latin for unconquerable.

[11] 'Fell' in this context means 'dreadful'. So the speaker is referring to the dreadful grip of awful circumstances. This could be argued to be a reference to the difficult circumstances which he found himself in during his illness.

[12] 'Fell' in this context means 'dreadful'. So the speaker is referring to the dreadful grip of awful circumstances. This could be argued to be a reference to the difficult circumstances which he found himself in during his illness.

[13] There is consonance here (repetition of the 'b' sound). This is not strictly alliteration, as the final 'b' is in the middle of the word. Hence, it's consonance.

[14] Again, this shows Henley's humanist leanings – the speaker's not blaming God or the Devil for his misfortune - it is 'chance' that has metaphorically 'bludgeoning' (beating) him.

[15] The speaker appears to be admitting here that (s)he has been hurt by the things that ahve happened is his/her life, but his/her head is 'unbowed', i.e. (s)he is still standing tall and refusing to allow those things to conquer him/her.

[16] This is a reference to the world – or this life – which has been a place of 'wrath and tears' because of the difficulties the speaker has been through. Using the preposition 'beyond', might imply that the speaker is talking about an afterlife, but the following line crushes that thought immediately with the idea that 'but' (meaning 'only') the 'shade' looms after 'this place'. 'Shade' used to be a term which could be used to refer to a ghost or disembodied spirit. It seems that the speaker is using it this way and saying that this would be a 'Horror'. There is no heaven in the speaker's philosophy.

[17] The 'menace' that the speaker refers to here is the ever-present spectre of death. The years pass by and bring it ever closer, but this iss all right by the speaker because (s)he is 'unafraid' (line 12).

[18] The word 'strait' here is an interesting one. Not only does it refer (in its slightly old-fashioned usage - think 'dire straits') to something that is difficult and challenging and also, in its other meaning, narrow (so a physically narrow gate), but it also rhymes with gate to make this line particularly cohesive.

[19] A gate is generally seen as a waypoint on a journey. People have argued that this is a reference to the Bible passage (Matthew 7:13-14) which reads 'Strait is the gate, and narrow is the way, which leadeth unto life, and few there be that find it'. This refers to the way to heaven. It seems obvious that this is a reference to this passage, but what the meaning might be is less clear. As Henley was a humanist, it seems strange that this is a reference to the Christian idea of heaven. However, the Bible quote only says 'leadeth unto life'. Although we can assume that this is probably the 'eternal life' promised in heaven, that doesn't mean that this is the sense in which Henley has taken it. Perhaps the speaker in this poem is using 'life' to mean a good, honest, full, rich life here on Earth. However, the speaker does say 'It matters not'. So perhaps this is a reference to heaven, but a rejection of it at the same time. It is an interesting point that you may wish to debate with the children.

[20] This is another reference to religion. It could be a reference to the Egyptian practice of provided a dead person with a funerary text (known to us now as 'The Book of the Dead') in scroll form. These scrolls detailed the trials the dead person's soul would have to undergo on the journey to the underworld.

[21] These two repetitively phrased lines show the strength of character of the speaker. (S)he is taking full responsibility for his/her fate and the state of his/her soul. The nouns 'master' and 'captain' are very strong and proud titles of a person of influence. The combination of the two shows that the speaker is feeling completely sure of him/herself. It reinforces the humanist message - there is nobody in charge of this person but the person him/herself.

Jabberwocky, by Lewis Carroll

'Twas brillig, and the slithy toves
Did gyre and gimble in the wabe:
All mimsy were the borogoves,
And the mome raths outgrabe.

"Beware the Jabberwock, my son!
The jaws that bite, the claws that catch!
Beware the Jubjub bird, and shun
The frumious Bandersnatch!"

He took his vorpal sword in hand:
Long time the manxome foe he sought
So rested he by the Tumtum tree,
And stood a while in thought.

And, as in uffish thought he stood,
The Jabberwock, with eyes of flame,
Came whiffling through the tulgey wood,
And burbled as it came!

One two! One two! And through and through
The vorpal blade went snicker-snack!
He left it dead, and with its head
He went galumphing back.

"And hast thou slain the Jabberwock?
Come to my arms, my beamish boy!
Oh frabjous day! Callooh! Callay!"
He chortled in his joy.

'Twas brillig, and the slithy toves
Did gyre and gimble in the wabe:
All mimsy were the borogoves,
And the mome raths outgrabe.

Jabberwocky, by Lewis Carroll - Annotated

This poem is a wonderful one to help children learn about how language works. It is a nonsense poem, written by the author of Alice in Wonderland, Lewis Carroll (whose real name was Charles Dodgson). He was a mathematician and logician and he had a love of the nonsensical. There are lots of bizarre and crazy words in this poem which Carroll made up. Depending on how you interpret them, the poem can mean several different things. The poem can be used for several purposes:

Looking at the unknown words, you could ask the children to provide definitions for them, based on the known words around them. Can they work out which are nouns, verbs, adjectives or adverbs?

You could ask them to re-write the poem, using standard English, replacing the made up words with real words, and see what effects they can create.

They could try telling the story of the poem in prose.

Having so many made up words in the poem helps the children to realize how much sense they can glean from a text in which they come across vocabulary they don't know. Perhaps it might be worth mathematically calculating what percentage of words are unknown to make the point that they can read tricky texts without worrying about understanding every single word.

Can the children use this as a stimulus to create their own nonsense words/sentences and explain what they mean? They can discuss the shades of meaning created by standard words and why their words are better or, if the word is totally new (representing something for which there is no English word) they can describe it and explain why we need a word for that.

Line no.	Rhyme scheme	Jabberwocky, by Lewis Carroll	Syllable Count
1	A	'Twas brillig, and the slithy toves	8
2	B	Did gyre and gimble in the wabe:	8
3	A	All mimsy were the borogoves,	8
4	B	And the mome raths outgrabe.	7
5	C	"Beware the Jabberwock, my son!	8
6	D	The jaws that bite, the claws that catch!	8
7	C	Beware the Jubjub bird, and shun	8
8	D	The frumious Bandersnatch!"	6
9	E	He took his vorpal sword in hand:	8
10	F	Long time the manxome foe he sought	8
11	E	So rested he by the Tumtum tree,	9
12	F	And stood a while in thought.	6
13	G	And, as in uffish thought he stood,	8
14	H	The Jabberwock, with eyes of flame,	8
15	G	Came whiffling through the tulgey wood,	8
16	H	And burbled as it came!	6
17	I	One two! One two! And through and through	8
18	J	The vorpal blade went snicker-snack!	8
19	I	He left it dead, and with its head	8
20	J	He went galumphing back.	6
21	K	"And hast thou slain the Jabberwock?	8
22	L	Come to my arms, my beamish boy!	8
23	K	Oh frabjous day! Callooh! Callay!"	8
24	L	He chortled in his joy.	6
25	M	'Twas brillig, and the slithy toves	8
26	N	Did gyre and gimble in the wabe:	8
27	M	All mimsy were the borogoves,	8
28	N	And the mome raths outgrabe.	6

Sonnet 27, by William Shakespeare

Weary with toil, I haste me to my bed,
The dear repose for limbs with travel tired;
But then begins a journey in my head
To work my mind, when body's work's expired:
For then my thoughts--from far where I abide--
Intend a zealous pilgrimage to thee,
And keep my drooping eyelids open wide,
Looking on darkness which the blind do see:
Save that my soul's imaginary sight
Presents thy shadow to my sightless view,
Which, like a jewel hung in ghastly night,
Makes black night beauteous, and her old face new.
  Lo! thus, by day my limbs, by night my mind,
  For thee, and for myself, no quiet find.

Sonnet 27, by William Shakespeare - Annotated

Originally, sonnets came from Italy and gradually evolved to mean a fourteen line poem with a regular rhyme scheme and rhythm. When sonnets first came to England, they were written in the Italian style; a style known as Petrarchan. Later, English poets, including Shakespeare, adopted and adapted the sonnet form into the most usual form known today, which is (perhaps unfairly, as Shakespeare did not invent it) known as the Shakespearean sonnet. Sonnets have a very specific rhythm and rhyme scheme. They are usually about love. Shakespeare wrote 154 sonnets, which were published after his death in a rough order decided by the publisher. They are all unnamed, aside from their number, and seem to be written to two different people (sonnets are usually addressed to the object of the writer's/speaker's love). One is a 'youth' and one is a 'dark lady'. The vast majority of the sonnets are written to the youth, with only the final 27 addressed to the dark lady (so this one is addressed to the 'youth'). However, as the order was not decided by Shakespeare, sonnets such as this one (where the addressee is not made clear) may in fact have been addressed to the 'dark lady', or even someone different entirely – it is impossible to be certain. The number of sonnets written for a man has led some critics to argue that Shakespeare must have been gay. However, there is no evidence of this. Shakespeare wrote in the voice of Romeo, the voice of Juliet, the voice of Hamlet and the voice of King Lear (to name but a few) in his plays. Why, then, do we assume that the sonnets cannot be an assumed voice also?

A Shakespearean sonnet has an abab rhyme scheme throughout, until the final two lines, which are a rhyming couplet.

A Shakespearean sonnet is written in iambic pentameter. This means that every line has ten syllables, broken down into five metrical feet consisting of two syllables each. A metrical foot in poetry is like a bar in music – it is how we separate rhythmic phrases of the same length. There are five metrical feet, called iambs, in each line of iambic pentameter. Each iamb is a unit of rhythm which goes 'da-DUM'. Thus, a line of iambic pentameter goes 'da-DUM da-DUM da-DUM da-DUM da-DUM', where each 'da' and 'DUM' is one syllable. A word such as 'away' has a natural iambic rhythm, because we put the emphasis on the 'way' when we pronounce it, we wouldn't say 'A-way', we would say 'a-WAY'. If you emphasise the natural rhythm of speech when you read a sonnet, you will notice the iambic rhythm immediately.

Line no.	Rhyme scheme	Sonnet 27, by William Shakespeare	Syllable Count
1	A	Weary with toil,[1] I haste me to my bed,	10
2	B	The dear repose[2] for limbs with travel tired;	10
3	A	But then begins a journey in my head[3]	10
4	B	To work my mind, when body's work's expired:[4]	10
5	C	For then my thoughts--from far where I abide[5]--	10
6	D	Intend[6] a zealous pilgrimage[7] to thee,	10
7	C	And keep my drooping eyelids open wide,[8]	10
8	D	Looking on darkness which the blind do see:[9]	10
9	E	Save that my soul's imaginary sight[10]	10
10	F	Presents thy shadow[11] to my sightless view,	10
11	E	Which, like a jewel hung in ghastly night,[12]	10
12	F	Makes black night beauteous,[13] and her old face new.[14]	10
13	G	Lo![15] thus, by day my limbs, by night my mind,[16]	10
14	G	For thee, and for myself,[17] no quiet find.	10

[1] The speaker has worked hard during the day and is physically tired (evidence for the fact that (s)he is tired in a physical sense is in line 2, wherein (s)he mentions having 'limbs with travel tired'). This may be seen as evidence that the poetic voice in not actually that of Shakespeare himself – as a writer, we could argue that his physical labour would have been minimal. That said, he would have been travelling between Stratford and London fairly regularly, so perhaps it's not work that's tired him out, but the journey.

[2] The adjective 'dear' shows that the speaker is thinking of his/her bed with pleasure. This implies that (s)he is really looking forward to being able to rest, further reinforcing the idea that (s)he is very tired.

[3] The first, literal journey over, the speaker now embarks on a metaphorical journey 'in my head'. This is a clever link between the first line and the third.

[4] Again, the physical is juxtaposed with the mental. Here it is work, where on the previous line is was a 'journey'.

[5] i.e. 'far away from where I live' – this embedded clause shows how far away the speaker's lover lives. Could we be seeing Shakespeare talking to his wife in Stratford? Could it be a metaphorical distance – perhaps a distance in class?

[6] In this context, 'intend' means 'decide to go on', i.e. the speaker's thoughts decide to go on a 'zealous pilgrimage' to see his/her lover.

[7] This is an interesting image. The speaker's thoughts are 'zealous', i.e. obsessive, fanatical – the implication here is that (s) he has little or no control over his/her thoughts. (S)he can't help thinking about his. her lover. This adjective, juxtaposed with the noun 'pilgrimage', which has connotations of religious worship, show how strong this relationship is and how much the speaker is dwelling on thoughts of his/her lover.

[8] There is a juxtaposition here between 'drooping eyelids' and 'open wide'. The implication here is that although the speaker is physically tired, (s)he is kept awake by his/ her racing thoughts. Again, the comparison is set up between physical and mental.

[9] There is a bit of context needed here – these days, it is extremely rare to be in complete darkness. However, back in Shakespearean times, there was no electric light and no streetlights. Candles would not have been left on all night. Therefore, when the speaker talks about 'darkness which the blind do see', although it is a metaphor, it is a very close representation of what (s)he would actually see - it would be utterly pitch black.

[10] This is a lovely metaphor; the sight of the soul! The sibilance between 'save' 'soul's' and 'sight' on this line and 'presents' 'shadow' and 'sightless' on line 10 works well also, to represent the quiet and hush of a dark night.

[11] In Shakespearean times, 'shadow' was synonymous with 'ghost' or 'spirit'. The speaker is saying that his/her lover's image appears before him/her, in the eyes of his/her imagination.

[12] This simile referring to the lover as a 'jewel' is lovely, because the speaker seems to be saying that their lover is what 'brightens up' their thoughts and their nights.

[13] The alliteration on 'black' and 'beauteous' reinforces the comparison between those two adjectives. In Shakespearean times, 'white' and 'fair' were compliments and 'black' and 'dark' were insults - it was an extremely racist age.

[14] Another direct juxtaposition of opposites; the speaker is implying that the night is brightened, beautified and made young by the imaginary image of his/her lover conjured by his/her thoughts.

[15] This is an exclamation of no real meaning – similar to the way we would say 'oh!' nowadays.

[16] The rhyming couplet at the end of a sonnet tends to summarise the main overarching theme of the poem. This phrase is a succinct summary of the poem's focus on the physical versus the mental.

[17] This is an interesting phrase. You could discuss this with the children - what do they think it means. Is the speaker separating 'myself' and 'thee' (i.e. his/her lover) in order to link one to the 'limbs' (from the previous line) and the 'mind' (from the previous line)? If so, which is linked to which? If we look at the order of the phrases, we would naturally link 'limbs' and 'thee', and 'mind' and 'myself'. However, this doesn't seem to make sense, when compared to the rest of the poem. If we link 'thee' and 'mind', it makes more sense. However, we could look at this another way. Perhaps both the limbs and the mind are both finding 'no quiet' because of both 'thee' and 'myself'. It could be that the physical tiredness and the mental disquiet are linked to effort that the speaker is making on behalf of their relationship (so on behalf of both him/herself and his/her lover).

The Tyger, by William Blake

Tyger Tyger, burning bright,
In the forests of the night;
What immortal hand or eye,
Could frame thy fearful symmetry?

In what distant deeps or skies.
Burnt the fire of thine eyes?
On what wings dare he aspire?
What the hand, dare seize the fire?

And what shoulder, and what art,
Could twist the sinews of thy heart?
And when thy heart began to beat,
What dread hand? and what dread feet?

What the hammer? what the chain,
In what furnace was thy brain?
What the anvil? what dread grasp,
Dare its deadly terrors clasp!

When the stars threw down their spears
And water'd heaven with their tears:
Did he smile his work to see?
Did he who made the Lamb make thee?

Tyger, Tyger burning bright,
In the forests of the night:
What immortal hand or eye,
Dare frame thy fearful symmetry?

The Tyger, by William Blake - Annotated

Line no.	Rhyme scheme[1]	The Tyger, by William Blake	Syllable Count[2]
1	A	Tyger Tyger,[3] burning bright,[4]	7
2	A	In the forests of the night;[5]	7
3	B	What immortal hand or eye,[6]	7
4	B	[6] Could[7] frame thy fearful symmetry?[8] [9]	8
5	C	In what distant deeps or skies.10	7
6	C	Burnt the fire of thine eyes?[9]	7
7	D	On what wings dare he[11] aspire?[9]	7
8	D	What the hand, dare seize the fire?[9]	7
9	E	And what shoulder, and what art,	7
10	E	Could twist the sinews of thy heart?[9]	8
11	F	And when thy heart began to beat,	8
12	F	What dread hand? and what dread feet?[9]	7
13	G	What the hammer?[12] what the chain,[12]	7
14	G	In what furnace[12] was thy brain?[9]	7
15	H	What the anvil?[12] what dread grasp,	7
16	H	Dare its deadly terrors clasp!	7
17	I	When the stars threw down their spears[13]	7
18	I	And water'd heaven with their tears:	8
19	J	Did he[11] smile his work to see?[9]	7
20	J	Did he[11] who made the Lamb make thee?[9]	8
21	K	Tyger, Tyger burning bright,	7
22	K	In the forests of the night:	7
23	L	What immortal hand or eye,	7
24	L	Dare[7] frame thy fearful symmetry?[9] [14]	8

[1] This poem has a very regular rhyme scheme, composed of twelve rhyming couplets. These are broken down into six regular quatrains (four line stanzas). The regularity of the rhythm is quite hypnotic, perhaps reflecting the awe the speaker seems to feel for the tiger by reflecting the regularity of rhyme of a song – or a hymn – of praise.

[2] This poem is written in trochaic tetrameter, with catalexis at the end of almost every line. What this means is that each line is composed of four metrical feet. A metrical foot in poetry is like a bar in music – it is how we separate rhythmic phrases of the same length. Tetrameter is the word for lines of poetry with four metrical feet in them. In trochaic meter, each metrical foot is made up of two syllables and the emphasis is on the first syllable. 'Tiger' is a classic example of a word with natural trochaic rhythm. In pure trochaic tetrameter, each line would have eight syllables and the rhythm would go: DUM-da DUM-da DUM-da DUM-da. However, Blake has used catalexis on the end of almost every line in this poem. This means that the final syllable of the last metrical foot of the line is missed off. Therefore, almost every line (there are six exceptions in this poem) has the following rhythm: DUM-da DUM-da DUM-da DUM.

[3] In contrast to the title of the poem, which is an impersonal reference to the tiger, this first line directly addresses the tiger. This increases the implication that this poem is in some way on ode, or poem of praise written to the tiger. The repetition is interesting – you could discuss with the children what they think it means. Is it repeated for emphasis on the name of the creature? Is it repeated because the speaker is so in awe of the beautiful creature (s)he is speaking to? Is it repeated to bring the reader's attention to the importance of the tiger?

[4] The alliteration here is nice; it emphasizes how much the tiger stands out against the darkness of the 'forests of the night'.

[5] Why the 'forests of the night'? Why not just the 'forests'? Perhaps the tiger is in some way a symbol of light and hope in the 'darkness' of the world (or 'forest'). Perhaps it's the complete opposite and the tiger represents the lurking threat in the darkness – the hidden evil burning where nobody can see it. Perhaps the ambiguity is deliberate and we are left to make up our own minds about what the tiger is – good or evil.

[6] The verb 'frame' here is very interesting. What does Blake mean by 'frame'? You could discuss this with the children. Perhaps this is 'frame' as in create the frame for – i.e. create. This would link nicely with the adjective 'immortal' on the previous line, as the only entity who is credited with creation of the world and all the creatures in it is God. However, there are several layers of meaning here. Perhaps Blake is questioning whether it is God's work and suggesting that it may be the work of the devil, as the tiger is perhaps a representative of evil. Blake was a religious person, so it is unlikely that he truly believes that the devil was the creator of the tiger. However, he is putting it out there in this rhetorical question to cast doubt on the question, make the reader question and consider the existence of evil the world. The devil is another 'immortal'. This reinforces the impression that Blake is questioning whether the tiger is good or evil. Then again, perhaps Blake is talking about himself. Who is daring to frame the tiger? Well, Blake is, with his poem and his art (Blake was a wonderful illustrator and engraver). Perhaps there is yet a third meaning for 'frame' - perhaps Blake is referring to capturing tigers and putting them in cages, where the bars act as 'frames'.

[7] This is a very interesting shift between 'could' and 'dare'. The first stanza is repeated work for word as the final stanza, apart from this one change. You could discuss with the children what the change means. What is the effect of changing this verb? 'Dare' is much more adventurous, of course, but it is also implying that 'framing' the tiger is in some way a daring thing to do - a liberty taken, perhaps? Maybe the person in the first stanza who 'could' is not the same as the person in the final stanza who 'dares'. Who could they be? It would be interesting to discuss this with the children.

[8] This half rhyme is interesting for several reasons. You could argue that it deliberately breaks up the poem's flow, implying that the 'symmetry' of the poem has been compromised and thus the symmetry of the image of the tiger which Blake is creating with his words. There is also the implication that the symmetry here is between good and evil - that the tiger is a perfect balance between good and evil; a natural creature with no malice or cruelty, but one which is ferocious and dangerous. (This would make sense of the adjective 'fearful' too.)

[9] The poem is formed primarily of rhetorical questions. This is a very speculative poem, which prompts the reader to ask questions too. Starting with the creation in the first stanza of a query over the nature of the tiger and whether it could be representative of good or evil, there is a thread throughout the poem of questioning as to where the tiger has come from; who has created it, why and what the purpose of the tiger really is.

[10] Again, this is a juxtaposition of the ideas of heaven and hell; 'deeps' is a fairly obvious reference to hell, where heaven is often referred to as being in the 'skies'.

[11] Who is this 'he'? Is this God? If so, there ought really to be a capital letter for 'he', as this was the standard practice for words referring to God right up to the 20th century (and sometimes is still used).

[12] There are lots of images related to being a smith here. The tiger seems as if it has been forged in a smithy. Again, this is a reference perhaps to a creator God or maybe to the devil. The speaker seems to be asking about the nature of the creator - perhaps we can also spy a reference to Blake himself again here. Is it Blake's work in creating the poem that he is talking about having forged?

[13] This could be a reference to either the twilight of the old day or the dawn of a new day, i.e. when light appeared on the earth from the stars. This could be a reference to the Book of Genesis in the Bible, where the 7 Day story of creation is told. Is this when the stars came out on the first night after the creation of the animals on Earth? Or the following morning? There is something fairly violent about this metaphor - either because it's the 'throwing' of spears, or because it seems like perhaps the stars are surrendering. Is this another Biblical reference to the war between the angels, where Lucifer (the devil) was thrown out of Heaven. Lucifer's name means 'light' - it could be that Blake is referring to him as a metaphorical star, who has thrown down his spear, because he has lost the war in heaven. The war in heaven happened before the 'fall', i.e. before Adam and Eve left the Garden of Eden. Perhaps, therefore, Blake is using the tiger as a metaphor for the beginning of evil or for the balance of good and evil. Evil came from the sin that Adam and Eve first committed.

[14] Who is this 'he'? Again, it's ambiguous. At first glance, it seems obvious that it's God – 'he who made the Lamb'. However, Blake wrote 'The Tyger' for a collection of poems called 'Songs of Innocence and Experience'. In this collection was a poem called 'The Lamb'. It is the counterpart to 'The Tyger'. So again, this could be a reference to Blake himself.

ABOUT TT EDUCATION

TT Education is leading the way in the development and delivery of innovative educational training and products, which make a difference through raising standards in primary schools. Our mission is to motivate and inspire primary teachers, school leaders and children to achieve outstanding results and outstanding schools through engaged learning and visionary leadership.

OTHER PUBLICATIONS FROM TT EDUCATION

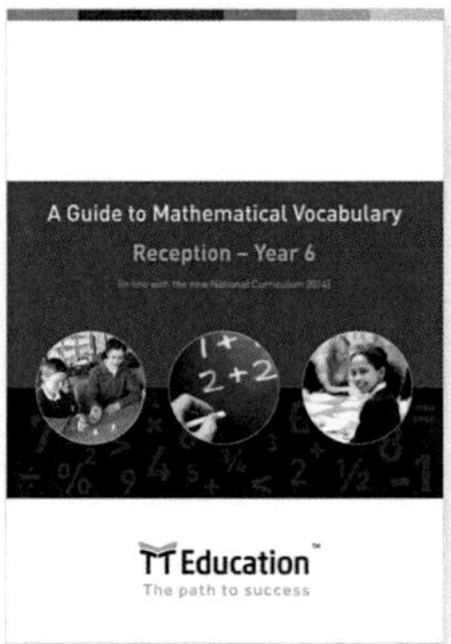

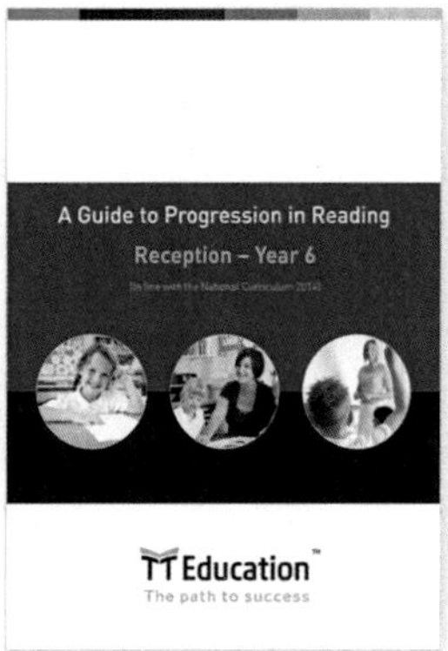

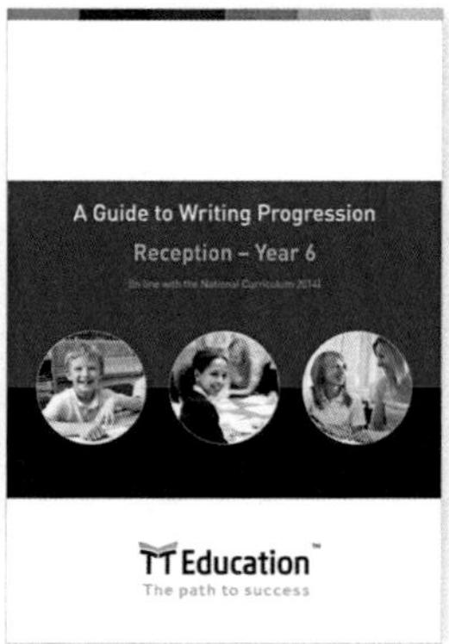

Fun with Non-Fiction

Fun with Non-Fiction is an inspiring collection of tailor-made model texts and teaching tips for every primary school year group. Designed to be funny, informative and engaging, with each text containing age-appropriate vocabulary, punctuation and grammar, this book with put the fun back into non-fiction lessons.

Guides to Progression

Our highly acclaimed Guides to Progression provide teachers with a clear framework for planning. Written by current practitioners, for current practitioners, all of these documents are fully aligned with the Primary National Curriculum. Each guide is broken down by year group and by skill, enabling teachers to see at a glance where their children are coming from and aiming towards. User-friendly and designed for planning purposes, this guide will prove invaluable in today's classroom; giving clear examples of what each skill looks like in each year group.